NO MORE SQUARE PEGS

HOW TO HIRE WINNERS FOR YOUR BUSINESS

Rob McKay

Hurricane Press
books that blow you away

AssessSystems

Physical address   Mailing address
1 Pupuke Road   PO Box 31544
Takapuna   Milford 0741
Auckland   Auckland

Phone: +64 (9) 414 6030
Fax: +64 (9) 414 6957
Skype: AssessNZ
www.assess.co.nz
Email: office@assess.co.nz

This edition published in 2011 by Hurricane Press Ltd
PO Box 568, Cambridge 3450, New Zealand
www.hurricane–press.co.nz
Email: info@hurricane–press.co.nz

Copyright © 2011 Rob McKay

Cover image: © Robyn McKenzie | Dreamstime.com

National Library of New Zealand Cataloguing in Publication Data

McKay, Robin, 1948-
No more square pegs : how to hire winners for your business /
by Rob McKay..
ISBN 978-0-9864684-5-2
1. Employees—Recruiting. 2. Employee selection.
I. Title.
658.311—dc 22

Printed by Bookbuilders, China.

CONTENTS

About the author

Author Rob McKay is one of New Zealand's leading authorities on the process of employee recruitment. He's the founder of AssessSystems, an Auckland–based consultancy that provides systems, tests and coaching to companies committed to hiring the best people. Rob has a BA in Business Psychology and an MA (Hons) in Industrial & Organisational Psychology from Massey University, but combines his knowledge with many years of hands–on business experience. He spent more than 25 years owning and managing radio stations on both sides of the Tasman, in an industry dependent on people performance.

What business leaders say about *No More Square Pegs*

'Compulsive reading for all who hire . . . the strategies in this book saved me so many times.' — *Brent Impey, former CEO, Mediaworks.*

'Great practical advice, easy to read and seriously handy.' — *Marc Burns, General Manager Human Resources, Canon NZ.*

'If you're responsible for hiring staff, read this book now.' — *Diane Foreman, CEO Emerald Group and 2009 NZ Entrepreneur of the Year.*

'I have become a firm advocate of using psychometric testing. Why? Because it works! Chapter 6 is a must read.' — *Sir David Levene, Chairman Quadrant Properties, and laureate of NZ Business Hall of Fame.*

'A brilliant tool for managers new to recruiting.' — *Marilyn Manning, Human Resources Manager, Les Mills New Zealand.*

1. MAKING THE RIGHT DECISION

People are your most important asset

Hiring new people is a chore. Smart business owners have realised the pitfalls of hiring people based on emotion, 'gut feeling' or the recommendation of others. So get it right the first time. Here's how to make the winning choices.

The cost of making a bad decision

In recent years, the quarterly staff turnover rate for all New Zealand business is 18.8% on average, according to the Department of Statistics. The cost to business to replace those who leave ranges from 25% to 50% of the employees' annual wages. For managerial and professional positions, the cost of replacement can run as high as the whole of the annual salary or more. About 80% of the real cost of staff turnover is hidden. Because those doing the hiring don't necessarily see the physical results of a poor decision, it is easy to lose sight of the impact on the bottom line.

Staff turnover is driven by two key factors — bad treatment, whether perceived or not and bad hiring decisions.

Responsibility for staff turnover and business failures sits firmly on the shoulders of those responsible for employing staff. It all starts at the top — the board of directors who hired the

Chief Executive Officer, and the CEO who hired the executives as well as the managers who hired the down–the–line staff.

Why do employees quit or fail in their jobs?

1 Most individuals who quit within six months were hired through an inadequate staff selection process — there was no structure and hence, no 'job fit'. There is a job for every person; the critical component to job success is whether the employee 'fits' the job role. Usually, when employees fail to perform, it is not the employee's fault. The hiring manager is to blame. She chose the wrong person.

2 Those that quit six to nine months into the job usually had poor staff orientation or initial induction training. In today's competitive business world managers are continually pressured for instant results. Many new employees are 'thrown to the wolves' and expected to deliver immediately. Often they can't, particularly sales people. Yes, they may have sales ability, but it takes time to understand a new organisation's products, customers and culture.

3 Those who quit between nine and 12 months were not given a realistic job preview, in other words, right at the start of the selection process management did not fully explain what the job was about and what was expected — they were 'sold' on the position. Once again, this is often true in sales roles. Promises of money and quick promotions that don't eventuate are a sure–fire way to lose talent.

4 Those who quit after 12 months have experienced poor leadership and management. It was the boss who was poorly recruited! As I said up front, an organisation with high turnover and poor results usually has poor leadership. The high turnover usually occurs first and can drift on for years, but will eventually impact on the bottom line. The board of directors starts asking questions. The leader fends this off with a multitude of reasons. But in the end, if the leadership hasn't got the right people on the bus it's the leadership that should go.

Why is it so easy to hire a horror story?

Many business owners and managers spend valuable management time trying to coach and train the new employee into the role or, realising their mistake, spend many painstaking hours attempting to manage the poor performer out of the position.

Worse still, many managers ignore the poor performance problem hoping it will go away, or get better. It never does.

Many hiring managers have the illusion that it's easy to hire someone, believing they have an ability to 'read people'; they can pick the right people instantly by the way they present and communicate. In other words they rely totally on gut instinct, first impressions, or worse still, personal bias and stereotyping.

Are you guilty of practising these selection prejudices?

— Fat people are lazy people
— Those kinds of people can't be trusted
— Short people make poor leaders
— People with weak handshakes lack assertion/confidence
— A woman would be too emotional for this position
— A woman with a young family will be unreliable
—Dirty shoes correlates with poor organisational skills
— Men with earrings are gay — gay workers cause problems
I'm sure you could add to the list!

There's nothing wrong with gut instinct as a final persuader, providing you have gathered all the evidence and weighed up all the options with a solid base of investigative research. It is easy to hire someone on emotional intuition — but are you prepared to take this gamble knowing it is almost impossible to reverse that decision without a drain on management time, employee moral and money?

The problem with the traditional hiring process is that it is usually performed under the pressure of time. We need to find someone now! This leads to short–cuts and emotional decisions based on how the manager 'feels' about the candidate.

An unstructured approach allows emotive decisions to be made unchecked, without any real consideration as to the candidate's ability to perform satisfactorily within the group of competencies — the performance factors critical to the job's success. (More about 'competency development' in Chapter 3).

Hiring a good performer is not easy. In today's job market many managers are finding it difficult to attract any applicants, let alone those that have the knowledge, skills and abilities to do the job. A retail store manager quipped to me during a recent seminar, 'the next applicant that walks in, if they have a pulse I'll hire them.' Frightening, but true. In today's job market, competent employees at any level are hard to find.

Having said this, the 'employee ocean' is not full of barracudas. You have to change your recruiting methodologies to deliver the right catch. Gone are the days when we could just bang an advertisement in the local newspaper and get flooded will a host of strong applicants. Recruitment advertising is not working in the same way it did before.

When it comes to recruitment, gone are the days of being

the hunted; successful organisations realise when it comes to finding the best talent, they are the ones that have to go hunting.

The truly successful recruiters think outside the square. Recruitment is an ongoing process. The trouble with many organisations is they wait until they have a vacancy before deciding to start looking for a replacement — more on proactive recruitment in the next chapter.

Few managers have been trained in the selection process. Many base their methodology on how they were hired. Many have no systemised process and as such rely on a 'hit and miss' approach.

During my years in this business I have identified a distinct pattern. When I talk to people about what we do at AssessSystems I get a lot of positive reaction:

'You guys must be in great demand; everybody needs to know how to hire the right people first time.'

'With today's employment laws we can't afford to make a mistake, your services would be really helpful.'

Or, 'Now I understand psychological profiling and have experienced its power I can't understand why more businesses don't use these tools.'

The fact is, most managers feel selecting the right person first time is an easy process, albeit time consuming. 'Why spend a few bucks getting our applicants assessed? Why spend $150 on background checking etc? I know how to pick competent people'.

Nobody can 'pick' or 'read' people and their abilities to perform the job through casual one–hour chit chat. This is a lazy excuse for a job interview. In most cases our clients come to us because they have failed in their previous attempt to 'read' the last employee and this has cost them dearly, both in employment grievance dollars and valuable management time.

Some hiring managers have no time to do it right first time, but somehow find plenty of time (and money) to do it poorly over and over again!

Unfortunately, when it comes to recruitment, most businesses are more consumed with meeting the budget than giving forward consideration to how they actually select their most precious assets, their people. If managers spent more time, effort and (here's the off–putting part for many) a little bit of money up front in setting up a standardised hiring system, those budgets would be delivered more often and with less stress. Competent, motivated staff is the differentiating factor in any successful business, no matter what the size.

What are the common hiring mistakes?

How do you rate yourself as a hiring manager? Here is a list of the most common mistakes made before and during the hiring process — not in any order or an extensive list. Are you guilty of any of these sinful hiring practices?

1 **Hiring under pressure.** Recruitment is an on going process. Too often, hiring managers think about potential applicants only when a staff member gives notice. Recruitment is continuous, especially for high turnover roles like sales, call centres, hospitality and retail.

2 **Replacing staff unnecessarily.** When an employee gives notice this is not an automatic signal to replace. Here is an opportunity to evaluate your business and restructure the job role. Ask yourself, 'Is there a need to replace this position?'

3 **Hiring close to home.** Hiring family members and buddies (or friends of buddies)? Yes, sometimes this works, if you're the Mafia, but most of the time it's a dangerous practice — nepotism and business are a poor mix. You are not a government agency hell bent on wiping out unemployment!

4 Unstructured interviews. Do you conduct unstructured one–on–one chit chats? Unstructured interviews are the most expensive and least valid of any hiring tool, yet the most popular. We cover interviewing in depth in a later chapter.

5 Poor reference checking. Are you guilty of not having a structured and disciplined reference procedure? Once a hiring manager has gone down the long path of vetting candidates and has decided who they want to hire, the last thing he wants to hear are negative comments from previous employers. Are you guilty of only listening to the positive points and fooling yourself that the negative areas can be easily addressed, or fixed?

6 Narrowing the field. Do you concentrate on a narrow source of recruitment avenues? To catch the best and biggest fish you have to cast your net wide. Relying on the situation vacant ads in the newspaper or a posting on an internet job site is not the panacea to recruitment. Once again, it's usually the most expensive and dirtiest pool to fish in!

7 Deciding what you really want? Do you know the performance factors (competencies) you want your new recruits to have? Many hiring managers dive into the hiring process without any documented guideline of what they are actually looking for in the new recruit. There is a total lack of planning. Winging it seems to be the common approach.

8 Fixed thinking. Are you guilty of stereotyping in your recruitment process? Many hiring managers have a predetermined mindset on the 'type' of person that can do the job — usually a person that is similar to them. This tends to negate older people, young women, women with children, people with disabilities etc. Think outside the square. In many cases, hiring on attitude and not aptitude works best in non–technical roles. It is easy to teach people how to do a job — for example, in a sales role, we can teach people how to prospect, present and close, but it is difficult to teach optimism, resilience, assertiveness and willingness to confront opposition etc.

9 **Hiring on emotion.** This is what I call, 'candidate infatuation' or, in other words, hiring candidates who look the part, dress well, are pleasant and communicative. These attributes don't necessarily identify abilities to be successful in the job. Nice, easy to get along with people are not necessarily good performers.

10 **Bending the rules.** When you set up a structured hiring system in your business, never bend the rules. This has been the downfall of many well–intentioned managers. For instance, if the candidate is a friend of one of our trusted staff, do we need to spend money on getting them profiled? Can't we rely on their word? To keep it legal, everybody must be treated the same way and be subjected to the same process. Irrespective of who the applicant is. Always follow your set selection process. Remember you are trying to compare apples with apples!

11 **Getting stuck in the 'referring' syndrome.** Sometimes excellent candidates come through referrals. This shouldn't be negated, but there is a down side — 'like tend to refer like'. Diversity in the workplace should be encouraged.

12 **Lack of training.** Most managers have never had any formal training in the hiring process. For example, how to frame interview questions, how to conduct a behavioural based interview, how employee profiling works, how this can benefit the hiring decision or how to conduct a valid reference check.

⑬ Hiring on experience instead of ability. It's easy to identify if a person CAN do the job, but the resumé and interview will not identify HOW they will do it. This is the domain of employee profiling. Psychometric testing is covered in Chapter 6.

⑭ Talking too much during interviews. Managers tend to 'sell' the benefits of working for their business rather than listening for the benefits the candidate will add to their business.

The above 14 points should scare you into deciding to systemise your hiring practices. This applies irrespective of the size of your business or the roles for which you are recruiting.

I'm a great believer in hiring tough and managing easy!

The three opportunities

As business owners we have three opportunities to do something about our employees' work performance:

❏ Opportunity 1: Let the poor performer(s) go

This is an almost impossible task if the poor performance was not initially addressed and several months, or even years, have slipped by. It is also expensive and demoralising for the said individual and those that work with him or her.

Poor performance rarely gets better. Most of us hate conflict and it is too easy to avoid addressing an employee's bad performance. If poor performance is not addressed immediately it will get worse. You will become more frustrated and the employee will glide on thinking they are producing acceptable work.

When the situation is finally addressed, conflict usually escalates and managers are prone to act impulsively. Result, wrongful dismissal and several thousand dollars off the bottom line through a personal grievance claim! You get what you reward. If you reward poor performance by not addressing it, that behaviour will continue.

❏ Opportunity 2: Fix the poor performance

After you hire, can you improve performance with training? My short answer is 'no'. You can't train your way out of a bad hiring decision. You will be throwing good money after bad. If you have hired a poor performer, the sooner you face up to your mistake the less money you will lose. Take a good hard look in the mirror, admit you got it wrong and revert to number one above!

❏ Opportunity 3. Don't let the bad apple in

The easiest place to prevent a problem hire is at the front door. If you proceed through a structured hiring system your chances of hiring a horror story will be greatly reduced. You'll also find the process less stressful and more economical in time and money.

People fear what they will lose, rather than what they will gain, so my focus in this book is not about hiring the right people, but rather on avoiding hiring a horror story.

The classic trio

Although getting the right person is critical to the success of any business, most businesses still place heavy reliance on traditional hiring practices, what I call the 'classic selection trio':

❏ **A CV or resumé.** Forget them! At best they will show you only how good a writer the candidate or somebody else is! An Application Form is more efficient, it collects the information you want in a structured manner so you can measure 'apples with apples'. A CV only gives you the information the applicant wants you to have.

It has been estimated that 68% of CVs contain untruths.

❐ An unstructured interview

This is nothing more than a basic chit chat, with the employer doing most of the talking! Final judgement will always be based on emotion and 'gut feel'. As of today, promise yourself you have done your last 'coffee bar' interview. Interviews need to be structured and conducted by at least two interviewers.

❐ A cursory reference check

This is usually done at the end of the process. At this stage the hiring manager has made up their mind and only listens to the positive comments, dismissing negative issues as being 'able to be dealt with via management and training'. Reference checks become more valid when structured — more in Chapter 9.

Businesses, large and small, shortchange the hiring process because they think a more thorough, comprehensive process will be too costly, or time consuming. When it comes to hiring, the daily pressures of 'getting things done' takes precedence over spending time to apply due diligence to the process.

The cost of hiring the wrong person far exceeds the costs involved in following a comprehensive, systematic hiring process involving sound recruiting, astute screening, a validated employment test, a structured behavioural interview conducted by two or more people, and a diligent reference and/or background check.

Like fishing, if you understand the process, are disciplined and develop your skills, you'll be successful most of the time, not just some of the time. Avoiding hiring the wrong person has a two–way pay–off.

Obviously when the right people are 'on the bus' the business will be more successful because competent people are helping you develop your business strategy, applying the appropriate tactics that will produce the desired outcomes — a healthy profit margin. Even more exciting is that your employees will be highly motivated because they are successful in a job that allows them to use their knowledge, skills, experience and innate personality characteristics. They are doing something they love and when you love doing what you are doing, you tend to do it well. That's a win–win combination!

The tree analogy

A good visual way to understand the total selection process is by thinking of a tree. The fruits of the tree represent the knowledge, skill and experience to do the job. These three qualities are observable, coachable and trainable and as such, can be tested through a structured interview, responses on the Application Form or CV, through reference/background checking, skills testing and work sample tests.

The fruits of the tree represent what a person CAN do (see Figure 1).

The roots of the tree represent the candidate's values, attitudes, mental ability, motives and personality. These attributes are innate, that is, they are basically developed by the time we are in our late teens. Latest research tells us the child we see at age 3 will be the adult we see at 30, a frightening prospect if you have an unruly 3 year old!

Whilst we may have the ability to adapt our behaviour in specific situations, we will always revert back to 'home base'. The roots can only be tested through valid and reliable psychometric assessment (an employee profile) — such as personality, attitudes and mental ability tests. The roots of the tree represent who the person is. By understanding the roots we get a better understand of knowing HOW the candidate will do the job. Most managers will hire on the fruits, but usually

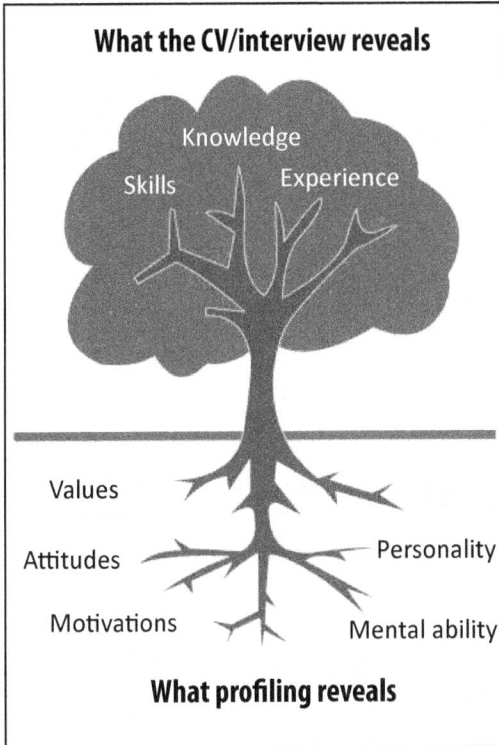

Figure 1: Resumes and interviews show you the
fruits, but profiling shows you the roots.

terminate, or have problem employees based on the roots of
the tree.

It's all about JOB FIT. Having the right levels of **S**kill, **K**nowledge,
Attitudes, **M**ental ability, **P**ersonality and **E**xperience (I have a
quick acronym for this, SKAMPE) will ensure the candidate is
successful in the role.

This is to the benefit of both the organisation and the potential
employee.

NO MORE SQUARE PEGS

2. THE SEVEN STEPS

A systematic selection process

Businesses usually have to select staff because of an internal promotion, resignation or dismissal of an employee, or the establishment of a new position.

A systematic selection process will increase the profitability of your business by:

❒ Ensuring you always compare 'apples with apples'. An unstructured hiring process is akin to measuring 'apples with oranges', great if you want to make fruit salad!

❒ Helping you to identify those candidates that don't 'fit' the job role.

❒ Ensuring all managers cover off all of the selection protocols during the hiring process thus avoiding rash hiring decisions based on emotion and gut feel.

As a rule of thumb in most businesses:

— 20% of staff are top performers.

— 60% are average performers.

— 20% are below standard.

(In Figure 2, overleaf, I've rounded the top and bottom segments up from 16% for easy comprehension.)

The challenge is to improve your talent pool during the selection process by:

❏ Screening out the bottom 20% of below standard performers. The hiring process is the most economical opportunity to exit poor performers! These people are sometimes hard to identify through the tradition selection methods as that are usually highly skilled at impressing you at interview — after all, they've had a lot of practice!

❏ Identifying the high performers and if necessary, average performers. It is impractical to think we can staff our team with nothing but high performers — statistically they are not available. However, average performers will not impact adversely on the business. Coaching and training them to better performance will improve the business.

The number one priority is to never, ever again, hire any of the 'twenty percenters.' These individuals drain your energy, drive away customers, alienate fellow employees, and demand a huge chunk of your personal time. In short, they cost thousands of unseen dollars.

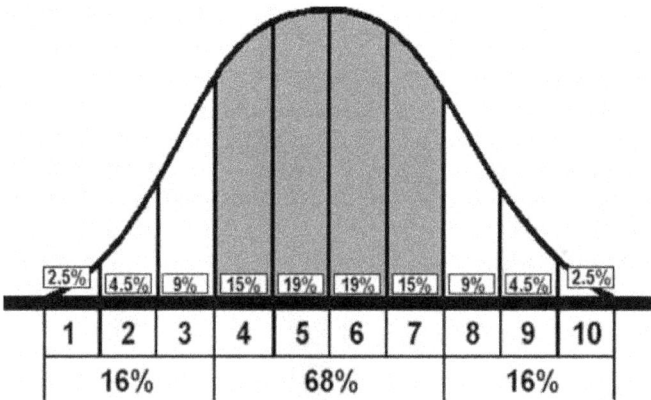

2.5%	4.5%	9%	15%	19%	19%	15%	9%	4.5%	2.5%
1	2	3	4	5	6	7	8	9	10
16%			68%				16%		

Figure 2: This bell curve demonstrates the distribution of top performers, average performers and under performers.

Remember, not all vacancies need to be filled

A vacancy provides an opportunity to ask these questions:

❐ Do we need this position? Charles Handy, the well respected British organisational psychologist, suggests that the outgoing person's tasks could be covered by an incumbent, but the employer should pay that person a third more.

❐ What does this position REALLY require? Now is the time to rework the position description. Can you adjust the original job tasks to add greater productivity to the organisation?

Do we screen in or out?

As explained above, a systematic hiring process involves a series of hurdles to filter the potential high performers from the marginal performers. The first hurdles result in screening out applicants who do not have the essential performance factors (the marginal performers). The next hurdles involve systematically screening out applicants according to whether they meet the desirable and bonus performance factors.

Selection techniques

There are many selection techniques that can be used to assess the essential, desirable and bonus performance factors (SKAMPEs). The 7 steps outlined in this book are not 'set in concrete'. Whilst you will implement all the steps in the process, the sequence may be changed to suit the type of position and the number of applicants.

Adopting a strategy of Screening Out unsuitable applicants is ideal for an entry–level position, if the number of applicants is likely to be large, or if many applicants are expected to have the skills required. Think of this process as having a jar of marbles. You only want the jar to contain red marbles. Your task is to select red marbles and discard the rest.

If the pool of applicants is small, if there is a shortage of skills or if the position is more senior, consider using a Screening In approach to look for the most suitable applicant. Now you have an empty jar, your job is to search the toyshops and try to source red marbles to add to the jar.

Screen Out Approach	**Screen In Approach**
Entry level positions	Middle to senior positions
Large number of applicants	Small number of applicants
Many skilled applicants	Shortage of skilled applicants

The selection process is like a tennis tournament in which players are systematically knocked out at each round.

The following table outlines the order of steps to be taken for both the Screening Out and Screening In approaches:

THE SEVEN STEPS

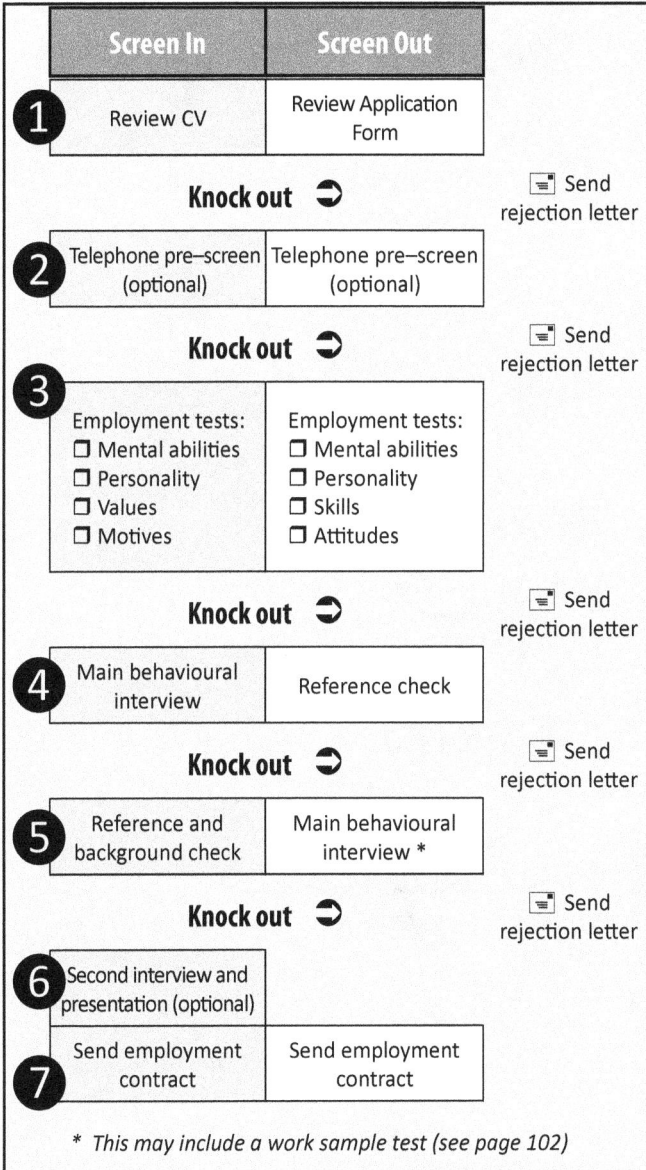

Screen In	Screen Out
1 Review CV	Review Application Form

Knock out ⟳   ✉ Send rejection letter

Screen In	Screen Out
2 Telephone pre–screen (optional)	Telephone pre–screen (optional)

Knock out ⟳   ✉ Send rejection letter

Screen In	Screen Out
3 Employment tests: ❏ Mental abilities ❏ Personality ❏ Values ❏ Motives	Employment tests: ❏ Mental abilities ❏ Personality ❏ Skills ❏ Attitudes

Knock out ⟳   ✉ Send rejection letter

Screen In	Screen Out
4 Main behavioural interview	Reference check

Knock out ⟳   ✉ Send rejection letter

Screen In	Screen Out
5 Reference and background check	Main behavioural interview *

Knock out ⟳   ✉ Send rejection letter

Screen In	Screen Out
6 Second interview and presentation (optional)	
7 Send employment contract	Send employment contract

This may include a work sample test (see page 102)

The seven steps to hiring

1 **DEFINE** the job and person required
— *job analysis*

2 **ATTRACT** the right applicants
— *recruiting*

3 **DO** the initial screening
— *application form, telephone interview*

4 **SCREEN** the high performers from the
average and poor performers
— *employee profiling*

5 **CONDUCT** the main interview
— *finding the 'company fit'*

6 **VALIDATE** information
— *reference and background checks*

7 **THE DECISION**
— *induction, initial training, legal*

Step One — Preparation

What are the specific SKAMPEs required for the vacant position? Remember these six key areas; I will refer to them often throughout the book. Many managers plunge headfirst into the hiring process without a clear written picture of performance factors required to be successful in the vacant position. Discussed in Chapter 3.

Step Two — Recruitment

How do you source, attract then identify applicants for your vacant position (Note, I will use the term 'applicants' for those persons initially applying for a position, but once they have progressed to the main interview I shall refer to them as 'candidates'.) Recruitment practices are addressed in Chapter 4.

Step Three — Initial Screening and Selecting Out

Eliminating unsuitable applicants from the application forms, CVs, and resumes can be supported by a brief telephone or face–to–face interview or, a more efficient approach, pre–screen applicants using a valid and reliable employee profile. The initial screen process is the subject of Chapter 5.

Step Four — Employment testing

The only way to understand the 'real' person before you hire. Usually tests personality, mental ability (for example, numerical, verbal or mechanical ability) and counter productive behaviours (attitudes).

By adding employee profiling to a structured interview, you will greatly increase your chances of identifying those applicants who don't fit the job. Employee profiling (psychometric testing) is covered in Chapter 6.

Step Five — The structured interview

Unstructured interviews are the most popular, but the least valid and therefore the most dangerous tool to use in hiring new employees. All interviews must be structured. Interview questions should be aligned to specific job competencies, be behavioural and/or situation based, multi–rated with at least two people conducting the interview. This process is outlined in depth in Chapters 7 and 8.

Step Six — Reference checking

Not doing a diligent reference check can spell disaster, doing it and negating negative information can be just as bad. Sometimes during reference checking we can hit the 'informational brick wall'. Chapter 7 discusses some practical ideas to ensure your reference checks are valid and reliable. Helpful hints are included in Chapter 9.

Step Seven — The decision

Methods for final decision making will include additional measures to separate similar candidates, such as work sample tests, second interviews and mock presentations. We also take a brief look at the employment contract and introduce you to the job induction process. These are explained in Chapter 10.

3. UNDERSTANDING THE JOB

Step 1: Preparation — who do you need?

As outlined earlier, the content of all jobs can be explained through the combination of Skill, Knowledge, Attitudes, Mental ability, Personality and Experience. When selecting new employees, you must have a clear understanding of the SKAMPE required for the specific job role you intend filling.

This table demonstrates how SKAMPE explains the functioning of a particular job. As an example, I have chosen a receptionist and retail sales position.

The job — receptionist	
Skill	Performs admin tasks with minimum error — good typing speed.
Knowledge	Can operate computer, phone system — understands Microsoft Word.
Attitude	Punctual, honest, reliable.
Mental ability	Strong verbal ability.
Personality	Service orientation, stress tolerance, outgoing.
Experience	3 years similar employment, certificate in Office Administration.

The job — retail sales person	
Skill	Is proficient at applying the sales cycle — can demonstrate closing tactics.
Knowledge	Understands the sales cycle — one aspect is closing the sale.
Attitude	Ethical, trusting, respects diversity.
Mental ability	Basic numerical skills.
Personality	Optimism, resilience, influencer.
Experience	2 years retail selling with preference for clothing sales

*Above: This applies the SKAMPE method to a position
of receptionist and retail sales person.*

Identifying performance factors (competencies)

Performance factors are the selection criteria or standards for a position. They are the core SKAMPE that a person needs in order to succeed in the position.

Before we start recruiting we need to do a job analysis which will identify the core SKAMPE for the role. In the world of work there are about 50 performance factors (competencies). It would not be practical to try and assess every single performance factor required for a job.

For this reason it is acceptable to narrow this down to a core group, usually between 5 to 10. In other words, what are the critical performance factors that are most important for success for this specific job?

Performance factors are usually divided into three categories:

❒ The **ESSENTIAL** Performance factors — these are the 'Must Haves'.

❒ The **DESIRABLE** Performance factors — these are the 'It would be nice to have', but not a total prerequisite for hiring.

❒ The **BONUS** Performance factors — these are the 'could have' qualities. They would add value to the organisation, but are not fundamental to the position. They are the 'icing on the cake'.

Essential Performance factors are known as 'knock out' factors as they describe the minimum job requirements the candidate MUST have, usually innate. Applicants not meeting the 'knock out' factors are not considered for the position.

If the skill can be quickly and easily developed in the workplace, it can be classified as a desirable rather than an essential performance factor. These are learned behaviours.

As an example, the following table demonstrates some performance factors that would be essential, desirable, or a bonus to a sales role.

Performance factors for a sales representative

Essential	Desirable	Bonus
❒ Customer focus	❒ Sales knowledge	❒ Computer savvy
❒ Presentation skills	❒ Sales experience	❒ Graphic design
❒ Negotiating ability	❒ Product knowledge	❒ Event management
❒ Communication skills	❒ Network of clients	
❒ Resilience		

Define the position and the person required

The first step in getting the right person for the position is to ask two questions:

☐ What are the key tasks and responsibilities of the position?

☐ What core SKAMPEs are needed?

Both these questions will be answered by completing a job analysis. The outcome of the position analysis is two fold:

☐ A position description.

☐ A person description.

How to do a job analysis

1 Review the present position description

If there is a current position description, check to see if it is still applicable. If not, update it by observing the person presently in the position, interviewing people connected to the position, and benchmarking against a similar position in another organisation — they may have a better way to achieve the outcomes of this job.

2 Observe the position

If possible, observe a person doing the job. Ask yourself the following questions:

☐ What is the person doing?

☐ What skills and personal attributes does he or she have and what more are needed?

☐ What are the working conditions?

☐ Who does the person interact with?

3 Interview person(s) connected to the position.

If possible, interview key staff members in the role and others who work closely with the person in the position.

Use the following as a list of questions that you may choose from when interviewing:

Interview questions for position analysis

Exploring the position	Exploring the person required
☐ What is your position title?	☐ What level of education is required for the position?
☐ To whom do you report?	☐ What level of literacy is required?
☐ Who reports to you?	
☐ What are the main objectives of your position?	☐ What level of numerical skills is required?
☐ What budget are you responsible for?	☐ What level of verbal (written and oral) skills is required?
☐ What do you spend most of your time doing?	☐ What buying or sales skills are required?
☐ What tasks need to be done?	
☐ Which tasks are most important?	☐ What computer skills are required?
☐ Who do you communicate with most?	☐ What level of physical fitness is required?
☐ What forms of communication do you use?	☐ What level of mechanical skills is required?
☐ What physical work is involved?	☐ What personal characteristics are needed to do this job well?
☐ What decisions do you have to make?	☐ What problem–solving skills are needed?
☐ What demands are made of you?	☐ What level of creativity is needed?
☐ Is there any travel involved in the position?	☐ What other skills do you need to do this job?

This is designed for middle to lower entry level positions and is a fast, ideal way to get to the core of the performance factors you need to assess when hiring.

These also link to specific interview questions that will be addressed when we discuss Step 5 — The Interview.

How to decide what's really important

The simple Job Analysis Survey on the facing page is an example of how you can create a checklist of elements of a job, and rate them so you identify which are critical.

Place a √ beside the 5 to 8 most important aspects of this specific job. Think about the core competencies and behaviours needed to be done on an hourly, daily, weekly basis to ensure success in this position.

Before you tackle the survey, ask yourself this question:

'To be successful in this job one needs to . . .'

Job Analysis Survey

Job title:

Person making ratings:

— Identify and appropriately solve problems.

— Plan, organise and schedule work.

— Promoting and reinforce safe work environment.

— Maintain effective teamwork.

— Communicate effectively with others, verbal and written.

— Delivering quality work — be accurate and reliable.

— Manage time efficiently and effectively — be organised.

— Be customer–service orientated.

— Coach, train and develop others.

— Manage or supervise, motivate and assist staff.

— Make timely decisions and sound judgements.

— Be creative. Generate new ideas and suggestions.

— Do presentation to customers, clients.

— Persuade people to buy products or services.

— Good attendance and punctuality.

— Good follow–through on tasks and responsibilities.

— Have industry and product knowledge, and apply this experience appropriately.

— Follow rules and policies prescribed for the job.

— Care for and operate equipment properly.

— Be adaptable, adjust to changing situation.

— Build strong business relationships with clients/suppliers.

— Develop one's self — keen to learn new job functions and up–skill.

— Meet set goals, objectives and commitments.

— Display integrity — honest and trustworthy.

— Be resilient — handle stress, criticism and failure appropriately.

The position description

The information gathered by doing the Job Analysis Survey, observing the job and interviewing current jobholders now has to be written up into a position description.

New Zealand businesses please note: the Employment Relations Act 2000 makes it a legal requirement to have a position description.

A position description outlines the purpose of the job, the key factors required for a person to perform effectively in the position; as well as the expected results.

Does your position description include . . .
— *The position title*
— *Purpose of the role*
— *Reporting relationships*
— *Goals and objectives of the position*
— *Key tasks and responsibilities of the position*
— *Key knowledge, skills, abilities and attributes*
— *Key performance factors (from Job Analysis Survey)*
— *Performance standards (How performance is evaluated)*
— *Challenges to be addressed in this position*

Here's an example of a position description:

Title:
What is the title of the role?
Administration Assistant

Purpose of Role:
What is the main function of the role, how does the role fit into this organisation?
To be responsible for the general daily operations of the business.

UNDERSTANDING THE JOB

Reporting Relationships:
Who will the jobholder be responsible to, and to whom will they refer to for urgent decisions/advice if this person is unavailable? Give their names and positions.
Reports to the Business Owner (name), in lieu of this (who).

Goals and Objectives:
What is required of the jobholder in order to be successful in the role?
To carry out duties in a timely manner, with a low margin of error. To ensure customers are cared for with superior services.

Duties and Responsibilities:
What duties and responsibilities does the jobholder need to perform in order to fulfil the purpose of the role and achieve goals and objectives — provide a list?
❐ Talks with customers, does booking, places orders.
❐ Fills out contract forms, determines charges for services requested, collects deposits, prepares invoices, does banking and mail.
❐ Helps to coordinate workflow.

Key Technical Skills, Knowledge and Qualifications:
What skills, knowledge and qualifications (certificates etc) are essential to be able to perform in this role?
❐ A basic understanding of general bookkeeping.
❐ Computer literate (Microsoft Office and Outlook).

Key Performance Factors (Sometimes referred to as competencies):
What personal characteristics/traits are required for a person

to perform well in this role? Usually 5 to 8 core factors:

❏ Attention to detail ❏ Customer focus

❏ Problem solving ❏ Ability to work in team

❏ Integrity

Performance Measures:

How will performance in this role be measured? How will they know if they are doing well or poorly? When and how often will this feedback be performed?

❏ Positive customer feedback — via annual survey

❏ Punctuality

❏ Accuracy of accounts, invoices etc.

❏ Every 12 months via an internal performance evaluation meeting and 360 survey

Challenges:

What are the potential challenges that the jobholder may face in this role?

❏ The administration functions are untidy; this role needs a self–driven person who takes ownership of the administrative function.

Step One Reminders . . .

— *Performance factors MUST relate to the position.*
— *Performance factors MUST comply with legal requirements, e.g. the Human Rights Act.*
— *Don't hire anyone who does not have the ESSENTIAL performance factors.*
— *Only consider desirable performance factors if resources exist to develop (train) new employees.*
— *Do not let bonus performance factors replace essential ones.*

4. FINDING THE RIGHT APPLICANTS

Step 2: Let's start recruiting — who's out there?

Recruiting, sourcing, or attracting suitable candidates is one area of the selection process that is often given little attention. Many hiring managers bemoan the fact that there are no suitable candidates available, or they have had little reaction to their recruitment advertisements.

The lack of quality candidates inspired one of our clients to remark, 'I feel like advertising; help wanted, pulse needed!' In most cases the organisation is at fault for not casting the recruitment net wide enough, or having a clear understanding of the core performance factors needed for the job.

Recruiting new staff is analogous to going shopping without a shopping list:

❐ You don't get what you want.

❐ You buy what you don't need.

❐ It costs you too much.

❐ And you have to go back to get the things you missed out on.

There are four factors to consider in the initial recruitment phase.

❶ How much money is available?

The cost of advertising varies greatly, so do the many

alternative recruitment methods. The allocation of funds to market the position will often be governed by the job status.

2 How quickly does the position need filling?

Remember, it may be better to struggle on short–staffed than to fill the slot with someone who is short on performance.

3 How wide do you cast the net?

If the job is highly specialised you can narrow your recruitment focus. For example, if you are recruiting for a school teacher, you can target your marketing to the Education Review magazine. Compare this to hiring a General Sales Representative. Seeking applicants for this role usually benefits from a wider reach — a shotgun approach.

4 The exemption level.

Here we mean the minimum requirements candidates must possess at application stage. For example, our applicant field would be narrower if we required Retail Sales People for our electrical store who must have an Electrical Trade Certificate.

Having addressed the above factors, what tactics are you going to use? In a survey by Aon Consulting, the most used recruitment sources were:

❒ Employee referral
❒ Newspaper adverts
❒ Recruitment firms
❒ Campus recruitment
❒ Temp services
❒ Internet job boards
❒ Walk–ins
❒ Government employment services.

The pressure to fill the vacancy often leads to the traditional process of 'let's place an advertisement in the newspaper', then making a selection from a small pool of (often poor) candidates — a recipe for disaster. Many managers only address recruitment when it becomes a necessity, when a staff member gives notice, when panic sets in. Recruitment is an ongoing process, especially for a sales manager.

Start a 'red file' and continually recruit. Keep a list of potential candidates. When you are out and about always keep an eye open for potentially good people. Introduce yourself. Give them a business card.

Tell them you are always on the lookout for great people and if a vacancy occurs would they mind you making contact. Or better still, get their contact details and ask if it's OK to call them if you have a future vacancy — add this to your 'red marbles file'

Question: do you need to hire?

When a vacancy occurs, one important question needs to be asked: 'Do we need to replace this position?'

If the answer is 'yes', what are the replacement SKAMPEs we are looking for (addressed in the previous chapter)? How and where will we source the appropriate applicants?

Is this situation familiar? An employee has just given notice, they are leaving in two weeks, replacement action becomes a priority.

Before pushing the panic button you may want to take two steps back and justify the need. You now have an ideal opportunity to ask the important question, 'Do we need to replace this person?'

Now would be a good time to evaluate alternatives like:

❒ Re–organising the workload by redeploying existing staff.

❒ Offering overtime or extended hours of work to existing employees.

❏ Re–analysing the job, to determine which tasks can be eliminated, automated or outsourced.

❏ Transfer employees from other departments or branches on a temporary or permanent basis — they may prove themselves.

❏ Promote an employee from a different job area. This has proven successful in areas like sales. That super receptionist you have could be your next sales star.

❏ Contract the work out via temporary workers, or outsource through consultants.

❏ Use the Charles Handy (a respected British organisational psychologist) principle — cut the staff in half, pay existing staff one–third more and ask them to do twice as much! If there is a replacement consensus, recruitment can begin.

Attracting the best people

Once you know who you are looking for the next step is to decide how to attract these people to apply for the position.

The goal of recruitment is to ONLY attract those people that have the required performance factors needed for the position, not every Tom, Dick, or Harry.

The following issues need to be considered:

❏ Recruit internally or externally, or both? The former is often your best source.

❏ Recruit yourself or through an agency?

❏ Where and how to advertise the position?

There are advantages and disadvantages to each of these options.

The best option becomes clear after considering the following factors:

❏ Time.

FINDING THE RIGHT APPLICANTS

❏ Cost.
❏ Administration.
❏ Accessibility and availability of suitable applicants.

The following table gives an idea of the pros and cons of each method:

	Advantages	Disadvantages
Recruit yourself	❏ Less costly ❏ Confident that process is done properly	❏ Time consuming ❏ Additional administration ❏ Need to be aware of legal issues
Use an agency to recruit	❏ Large database of suitable applicants	❏ Costly ❏ Do you have confidence in information gathered (reference checking)? ❏ In their eagerness, many agencies put people in front of you who you'll like, but who can't do the job
Recruit internally	❏ Motivates staff ❏ You know person's track record ❏ Less costly	❏ May not get best person for the job ❏ May not cast your net wide enough and miss the special person who could add to your business
Recruit externally	❏ Get new insights and skills	❏ Don't know the person

Doing it yourself

Attracting applicants can be a major cost saver in terms of agency fees. However, the administrative costs of recruiting yourself are hidden. To manage these costs and streamline your recruitment process, follow these simple guidelines.

Here are some recruitment issues to consider.

Do you want to recruit internally, or externally, or both?

Many managers stereotype their current employees. Just because a person is a receptionist doesn't necessary mean they don't have the appropriate SKAMPEs to fit another position.

If the new position is not highly technical you may find an existing employee has the interest, the right attitude and the ability to excel in a new position. While I was managing commercial radio stations some years ago two women who joined the company as receptionists later became our best sales representatives.

It is easy to train and coach. It is impossible to change personality and adapt attitudes. With internal candidates you have the advantage of knowing them and they understand your organisation. A promoted employee becomes a motivated employee, and that adds up to better performance from that person and acts as an encouragement to their colleagues.

Recruit yourself or use an agency?

Many agencies are concerned with putting people in front of you that you will like but who may not necessarily have the ability to do the job.

Most agencies present a continuous stream of candidates in the hope that they will eventually present someone to justify their fees. The inherent problem is the way employment agencies and their consultants are remunerated. Most recruitment personnel have no formal HR training. They are sales people, and as such are driven by budgets and are remunerated by commission.

There are some good recruitment consultants around; the trick is to recognise the sharks and avoid them.

If you are searching for a recruitment consultant here are some tough questions to ask:

❑ What formal qualifications, training and experience does the individual consultant have in recruitment?

❑ What processes do you use, or go through before recommending a candidate to us?

❑ How are your consultants remunerated? If it includes a percentage of the placement monies, are they intent on meeting their goals or yours?

❑ What type of psychological assessments (job fit instruments) do they provide? Is this done internally or externally? If internally, what qualifications do the administrators have? Is the assessment valid and reliable? Does it have predictive validity, or is it just a type behaviour instrument like DISC or MBTI? These behavioural tools are ideal for team building, but totally unsuitable to use for selection. More about this in Chapter 6.

Here are some negotiation ideas:

❑ If an agency does the process, they should have no hesitation in refunding the bulk of you placement fee if the candidate is unsuitable after three months. Agencies have a 'so called' guarantee — 'We'll replace the 'failed' candidate with another at no fee'. Ensure your contract has a 'money back' clause.

❑ If you are only using the agency to put people in front of you, negotiate a fee that represents this referral. This is exactly what most agencies do — they hold databases of current and future job hunters. They are introduction agents.

☐ Few agencies conduct multi–rated behavioural interviewing, psychological testing and stringent in–depth reference checking. In any event you are still going to conduct your own selection process. I'd recommend doing your own structured interview, independent employee profiling and reference/background check.

Don't rely on agencies to do this diligently — remember most are there to 'clip the ticket'! Their personnel are not usually trained in HR, and sometimes are, at best, salespeople driven by placement targets.

Okay, so you want to do it yourself

This is always a balance between administration and convenience, between the known and the unknown, between effort and laziness. It's like fishing — do I catch it myself and have confidence in knowing I'm eating fresh fish? There was a cost for boat fuel, tackle and bait. And for our time, but we could class this as entertainment.

Or for convenience sake, do I go to the local fish'n'chip shop? Here, I pay cash up front, but there may be a hidden cost — an unsatisfactory taste or food poisoning. And no joy through the thrill of feeding the family.

There are two lazy ways to attract applicants: place an advertisement in the newspaper; or call up your local recruitment agency.

We would encourage you to cast your net as wide as possible, using a variety of recruitment methods.

Newspaper advertising

Let's start with one of the most common and least creative.

FINDING THE RIGHT APPLICANTS

The newspaper usually has good reach into the job market. A word of caution, as we have discussed previously, the bell curve (refer back to Figure 2 on page 20) reminds us of our 80/20 rule of work performance. That is, about 20% of your workers will be high performers, 20% low performers (your hiring mistakes) and the balance, 60%, will be seen as average.

Accepting the above analogy, one could assume the bulk of high performers are content with their current position, they are not looking to move, are not scanning the situation vacant pages of the local newspaper. These people are happy in their current position. To tap into this pool requires a more creative approach.

On the other hand, the poor performers are probably getting the 'squeeze' to perform better in their current position and, feeling the 'heat', are on the lookout for a new employer to accept their mediocre performance. The chances are, if your hiring process is not diligent you'll end up being the next sucker who gets saddled with this poor performer.

The above situation is particularly prevalent with sales and marketing positions. These candidates are masters at interviewing. Most have the 'gift of the gab' and if your selection process is unstructured and you do not check out the roots, (using employee profiling) you'll be swayed by their performance at interview. We'll address interview bias in an upcoming chapter.

Sales people are very good at selling themselves at interview, but not necessarily good at selling on the job!

If you intend advertising your position in the press your advertisement must get attention. It must sell readers on why your position and company is a desirable place to work. Use your logo and invest in some 'snappy' artwork.

Think about which newspaper best targets the people who you want to attract. With entry level positions, as mentioned above, the most reliable candidates live closer to their place of work; therefore the local 'throw away' may work better than the costly metropolitan.

If your business has high traffic, how about a prominent notice?

Some retail businesses use this recruitment method very efficiently. You could get very creative here. Customers that visit your premises are usually loyal customers and shop in your store because they believe in the quality, style, value and service provided. Some of these customers would probably have the right personality, attitudes and mental ability to sell your products, or know of friends who would be ideal for the job.

I'm not suggesting a blatant 'Help Wanted' notice — something subtler, something that will encourage word of mouth. How about, 'We are looking for a person with great customer service, initiative and personal drive. If you know someone who would enjoy servicing our customers tell them to contact us for more details etc.'

Think about distributing a similar notice in areas where potential candidates may gather. Ideas here could be your local gym, under car windscreens, university notice boards. What about handouts in and around your local area like malls, sports fixtures etc.

Your company newsletter

If you produce a newsletter, put an 'opportunities' notice in every month, even if you don't have a vacancy. Your aim is to build a 'prospective candidates' list so that when an unexpected vacancy occurs you have a starting base of candidates. How about a cheekier idea, a notice in your client's newsletters (non–competitive, of course).

Catalogues, menus etc.

Akin to the above, if you produce catalogues how about a notice saying 'we are always looking for good staff etc . . .' within the pages of the catalogue?

If you run a café, something subtle on the bottom of your menus may stimulate applications.

Internet

This has now overtaken the newspaper and certainly worth considering, depending on the job role. You have to ask the question, 'are the applicants we are targeting proficient internet users?' Recruiting for lower entry positions may not work well in this environment due to computer availability or literacy. Some suggested New Zealand sites are:

www.seek.co.nz
www.trademejobs.co.nz
www.netcheck.co.nz
www.nzjobs.co.nz
www.sjs.co.nz (for part time students)
www.jobuniverse.co.nz

Social media sites such as LinkedIn and Facebook are also powerful tools for finding suitable recruits.

Mailbox drop

Draw up a creative 'wanted advertisement' and distribute in local post boxes, or private home mailboxes. The latter are ideal for those businesses looking for housewives returning to work, for example, call centres. I've always found that using photographs and testimonials from current employees as the basis of the flyer works well with this tactic.

Email blitz to your network

Use your email address book: 'Do you know of anyone who may be interested in a position we have open?'

How about a note in your monthly accounts

'Do you know anyone who would be interested in working in our accounts division etc.?' A great way to reach administration prospects but you may upset some current clients!

Company signage

The best I've seen was on the rear window of a local Auckland refrigeration company's service vehicles. All their service vehicles had a 'we need great refrigeration mechanics now, call us for details etc...' What a fabulous idea and a great example of continuous recruitment!

In–store recruitment booth

I saw this idea in a Guess store in the United States. It was a small cubical inside the front doors — It had a large inviting sign — a call to action. There was a small table and chair, application forms and pens, plus a box to drop your completed application form in — sort of reminded me of a large voting booth. And yes, there was someone filling out an application.

Increase the pay and benefits

In a tight labour market attracting good employees is difficult. Many are satisfied with their current job. It's your job to make them aware of the added attractions of working for you. This will not always be money, but it sure helps.

Would you rather have one good performer earning above market rate, or two poor to average workers on minimum wages? There's a lot of truth in the old saying 'if you pay peanuts you get monkeys' — a reason the hospitality industry has such high turnover.

Apart from wages, desirable benefits can also be a good attractor. Some examples are:

❑ Medical and dental benefits

❑ Training and tuition fees

❑ Childcare help

❑ Club membership — gym membership adds to employee wellbeing

❑ Profit sharing and share options

❑ Paid holiday trip

❑ Motor Vehicle — Petrol allowance

❑ Food credits

Finally, here are some other creative thought starters:

❑ Your local business association.

❑ Radio advertising — expensive but good reach. Depending on your business you may be able to contra off your services or products for lots of station airtime.

❑ An airplane banner. Don't laugh, don't you always look up when you hear a buzz overhead? This tactic is ideal for summer to target the sun worshippers on local beaches. Don't do it on a week day — you may only attract those with poor company fit (attitude and reliability) who are cracking up a suntan on their boss' time!

❑ How about a billboard in a high–traffic area for a month?

❑ If your business has a prominent building, what about a

banner on the side of the building?

I'm sure your team could brainstorm many other recruitment avenues that could be more effective than the traditional internet and newspaper advertising, and may be at a better price — free.

The point is, don't concentrate only on the area where everybody else is fishing. To catch the big ones, move off the crowded beach!

Writing your advertisement

Outline the performance factors and other relevant details. Be specific; avoid broad, sweeping statements like 'Only people with attitude need apply'.

List the simple measurable core SKAMPEs you are not negotiable on — refer back to your Job Analysis — the core performance factors needed for this role.

Also include any special work conditions like hours and environmental conditions. Make your advertisement stand out. You are in competition with many other employers. What makes your position more attractive than your competitor's business?

You may also want to take an opposite stance and highlight the type of person you don't need, or perhaps some of the less glamorous aspects of the roll.

Factors to consider when writing an advertisement

❐ Who is your target market? Are you trying to attract school leavers, graduates, or present employees?

❐ What is the best and most cost efficient media to reach your target market? Newspaper, internet, radio, billboards, community notice boards, flyers etc?

❐ Will your target audience notice the advertisement? Are you using boxes, bold type, graphics, and catchy phrases?

❐ Is your advertisement sending out a realistic message? Are you telling it like it is, both the positive and negative?

It is an offence in terms of the Fair Trading Act to place a misleading advertisement.

❐ Does the advertisement tell applicants how to apply for the position? Should they phone, send in a CV, or complete an Application Form on your website etc?

❐ Does your advertisement use any discriminatory language? Unless you have a good reason, you cannot discriminate on the basis of gender, race or marital status.

❐ Put a date on when applications close or outline a time frame for the hiring process.

Decide who will administer applications

By now you have made a choice of media to use and, if needed, written your advertisement and compiled the job and person specifics for the position. Before venturing any further you will need to designate someone (and brief them) on procedures to:

❐ Deal with all the enquiries.

❐ Record the dates when applications/CVs are received.

❐ Communicate with applicants who progress. Set interview dates and times and set up employment tests etc.

❐ Send out acknowledgement letters and rejection letters at the end of the process. You may be dealing with a current or future customer — don't invite bad PR through word of mouth.

AssessSystems offers a tool on its website, with a 30–day test option, that makes it easy to manage the above tasks. It's called the AssessSystems Applicant Process System (APS).

Step Two Reminders . . .

— *Take a marketing approach to your recruitment efforts.*
— *Always cast your net wide — don't settle for the first person who walks through the door.*
— *Brainstorm ways to advertise your position. Don't just rely on a newspaper advert. Think outside the square.*
— *Consider using AssessSystems' web–based Applicant Tracking System. It automatically screens and tests applicants so you only have to interview those who 'fit' the role.*
— *Remember, most recruitment agencies are introduction agents. Do your own structured interview, employment testing and referencing. You will have much greater comfort in the outcome.*

5. INITIAL SCREENING

Step 3: Initial screening — application forms and telephone screening interviews

In Step One we defined the job, and explained what SKAMPEs are required to succeed in the role you are seeking to fill. We then transferred these into a job description. In Step Two we started attracting applicants. Through advertising, promoting, networking and marketing we built up a list of potential candidates. Now to Step Three — how will applicants apply for the position and how will we filter their applications?

The purpose of the initial screen is to select out applicants that would fall into the left hand side of the performance bell curve, the 20 percenters (see page 20). If you are not diligent, these poor performers can slip into the main interview process and chew up hours of valuable management time — in some cases their charm and presentation gets them hired, but charm and presentation does not always equate to performance on the job.

A word of caution: A strict pre–screening process may 'knock out' some valid performers, but there is a bonus, the chance of hiring a poor performer is greatly diminished.

Remember your goal is to look for eagles. There are a lot of turkeys out there masquerading as eagles. Many people have set up successful businesses teaching turkeys how to look and behave like eagles — companies that produce resumés, professional interview trainers and recruitment coaches. Even recruitment agencies 'school' their applicants on how to 'present' themselves to their clients.

Application form and CVs

In mid to lower entry level positions we recommend all applicants apply via a customised application form. About the only thing a CV can tell you is how good the candidate is at creative writing. Or for that matter, how good the professional is who was paid to construct it!

Resumés are often embellished with exaggerated job descriptions and sometimes with outright lies. The latter is often referred to as the Apollo Syndrome after an applicant claimed in his CV that he 'provided key support to the top scientists on the Apollo team'. He was actually the barista in the staff café. He believed if it wasn't for his coffee making skills the scientists would not have stayed awake long enough to get their craft to the moon!

CVs will address information in different formats making it difficult to compare one applicant to another. We suggest you design an application form that collects the information that you need to know to make decisions on who to progress forward in the selection process.

To assist you in making this decision it's helpful to make a list of 'knock out' points. These are areas that you have decided will not be conducive to success in this position. Be careful with this process as you can only differentiate between applicants based on the minimum requirements for the job.

For example, you can't knock an applicant out because they

have school–age children, or because they spent six months at their last job. However, many hiring managers do build knock out points around many illegal criteria: areas such as number of jobs in the last 18 months, how far from the place of work the applicant lives, or if they intend to start a family in the foreseeable future.

Research shows that many illegal knock out points do have correlation with performance and job tenure. But hiring or not hiring based on a presumption made because of a person's age, marital status or other personal factors is a mistake and illegal.

Of course there are many legal knock out points you can ask in you application form — some examples are:

❑ Do you have a legal right to work in New Zealand?

❑ Do you have a valid driver's licence and do you have any demerit point on your licence? This is acceptable if the job involves the use of a motor vehicle.

❑ What is your date of birth? — If the job requires the person to comply with the law, like working in licensed premises.

❑ We could legally discriminate on gender if the job was, say, a retail sales person for a women's underwear shop.

❑ Do you smoke? This is acceptable if the company has a no smoking policy.

To help you frame your knock out points, it's important to have a list of the Skills, Knowledge and Experience needed by the candidates to successfully perform.

Remember, an application form will only help you assess Knowledge, Skill and Experience. You can only see the fruits on the tree! We will check out the roots of the tree in the next chapter on psychometric testing.

It's not overly important to consider experience in sales unless the position is highly technical. You can teach a person to sell, but you can't teach those innate personality characteristics that drive sales success like resilience, optimism, motivation to influence and persuade (ego drive), assertiveness, willingness to confront opposition etc.

In designing knock out points, refer to your job analysis and your subsequent job description. You may also want to think about what you don't want candidates to have.

Don't fall into the trap of getting excited about overly qualified people. Ask yourself the question — 'why would this person apply for this job?' Overly qualified people don't last long; they get bored and move on to seek more challenging roles.

Hiring new employees is about discrimination. However, to discriminate fairly and legally you must treat all candidates the same way making sure the discrimination is based on the candidates' ability to fulfill the role.

The employment law forbids you to discriminate on gender, religion, marital status, sexual orientation, etc. Here are some basic guidelines. We urge you to check these with your own legal team as legislation in your country or state may vary.

Types of questions you may/may not ask in the selection process:

Name
Legal: To inquire whether the candidate's work records may be under another name.

Illegal: To ask for maiden name.

Address
Legal: To request place and length of current and previous addresses.

Legal: To ask for a candidate's phone number or how he or she can be reached.

Illegal: To ask if a candidate owns or rents their home or who resides with them.

Age

Legal: Require proof of age by birth certificate after hiring.

Illegal: To ask the candidate's date of birth.

Birthplace/national origin

Legal: None.

Illegal: To ask birthplace of candidate or that of his/her parents, grandparents, or spouse.

Illegal: Any other inquiry into national origin.

Race/colour

Legal: To indicate that the institution is an equal opportunity employer.

Legal: To ask race for 'affirmative action plan' statistics after hiring.

Illegal: Any inquiry that would indicate race or colour.

Sex

Legal: To indicate that the institution is an equal opportunity employer.

Illegal: To ask candidate any inquiry which would indicate gender (unless there is a genuine occupational requirement ie: a retail sales assistant in a lingerie store).

Religion/creed

Legal: You may inquire about availability for weekend work.

Illegal: To ask a candidate's religion or religious customs or holidays.

Illegal: To request recommendations from church officials.

Marital/parental status

Legal: Status (only married or single) after hiring for tax purposes.

Legal: Number of dependents after hiring for tax purposes.

Illegal: To ask marital status before hiring.

Illegal: To ask the number and age of children, who cares for them and if candidate plans to have more children.

Illegal: Provisions for childcare.

Education

Legal: To ask what academic, professional or vocational schools attended.

Legal: To ask what languages candidate reads, speaks or writes, if use of a language other than English is relevant to the job for which candidate is applying.

Illegal: Specifically ask the nationality, racial or religious affiliation of schools attended.

Illegal: To ask how foreign language ability was acquired.

Criminal record

Legal: To request listing of convictions other than misdemeanours.

Illegal: To inquire about arrests.

References

Legal: To request general and work references not relating to race, colour, religion, sex, national origin or ancestry.

Legal: To ask who referred the candidate for a position with your firm.

Illegal: To request references specifically from persons who might reflect race, colour, religion, sex, national origin, or ancestry.

Illegal: To request personal references of family members.

Organisations

Legal: To ask if the candidate has worked as a paid employee for the National Party, Service Workers Union, YMCA, etc., as it pertains to a candidate's experience.

Illegal: To ask the names of organisations that would indicate race, religion, national origin, sex or age.

Photographs

Legal: May be required after hiring for identification purposes.

Illegal: Request photos before hiring.

Illegal: To take pictures of candidates during interviews.

Work schedule

Legal: To ask willingness to work required work schedule.

Illegal: To ask willingness to work any particular religious holidays.

Physical data

Legal: To require candidates to prove ability to do manual labour, lifting and other physical requirements of the job (be consistent).

Illegal: To ask about height or weight impairment or other non–specified job–related physical data.

Physically challenged

Legal: To inquire if the candidate can perform the essential functions of the job that he/she is applying for with or without an accommodation.

Illegal: To exclude physically challenged candidates as a class on the basis of their type of disability.

Illegal: To ask the nature of the disability, severity of the disability, condition causing the disability, any prognosis or expectation regarding the disability, whether or not the person will need treatment or special leave because of the disability.

Pregnancy

Legal: None.

Illegal: To ask if the candidate is planning a family or if candidate is pregnant.

Note: Even if the pregnancy is obvious, the job cannot be denied for that reason by itself.

Employment status

Legal: Where were you working between July 1997 and February 1998?

Illegal: Have you ever been unemployed or on any benefit?

Once again, a good general guide is to stay away from any 'hurdle' processes, or interview questions that do not relate to the person's ability to perform the job. A good rule of thumb is, 'When in doubt, leave it out!'

When conducting the initial screening process you are not only looking and listening for the candidate's experience, knowledge and skill, but also what is not in the application form. Remember, the candidate is trying to present him/herself in the best possible light, so there will be some skeletons in the closet; your job is to find them. Here's a checklist:

A checklist for screening applicants

— Look for gaps in the chronology of the applicant's work history.

— Don't assume. Verify qualifications with relevant authorities. A PhD can be purchased on the internet. It's amazing how many managers accept educational qualifications. Also ask yourself if the educational achievements are appropriate to the job.

— Has the applicant pursued further education and training? This indicates a willingness to learn and improve oneself.

— Estimate time spent in each job. Is there a pattern?

— Ask yourself, 'Is this candidate making a logical career move?' Does the applicant's employment history seem logical and stable, and does it show growth?

— Are there specific achievements, strengths, or accomplishments highlighted for each job.

— Is it apparent why the applicant left each of their previous jobs?

— Does the resumé/application indicate organisation? (spelling, handwriting etc.).

— Align references with previous positions. Are any missing? Why? Also check that the phone number on the application matches that of the organisation.

— Is it apparent why the applicant wants this particular job or role?

Once you have screened out the applicants that don't fit your job description, send out rejection letters (emails/letters) immediately. This is very important; it profiles your organisation as efficient and customer–service driven.

The content of the rejection letter should be polite, but please don't feel you have to explain the reason for rejection, especially if the candidate phones you. A slip of the tongue, or a flippant remark could land you a personal grievance. You are not required to justify your decision.

Suggested rejection letter

Thank you for applying for the position of (job title) with (company).

We appreciate your desire to work for our organisation and the effort you put in to the application process. Unfortunately we do not have a position that matches your knowledge, skills, abilities or experience at this time. Should you wish to apply at a later date we will gladly reconsider your application.

May we take this opportunity to wish success in your future and thank you for considering (company) as a potential employer.

Realistic job preview

Many employees leave after within 90 days because the job was not what they expected. The best time to sell and explain the job is before you waste valuable management time in the selection process. The ideal place to re–address the job description is at the application stage. A good idea is to print the job description on the flip side, or attach it to the application form. Another suggestion it to post it on your website.

Once the application phase has closed (put a date on this in your recruitment marketing) and you have selected the appropriate applicants to move forward, it's time to progress to the first interview screening.

Assessing application forms and brief telephone interview

The first step in the selection process is to 'knock out' those applicants who do not have the essential performance factors, by assessing all applications.

To ensure that each application is systematically analysed, draw up a matrix of the three categories of performance factors. Assess the contents of each application in terms of these categories. This matrix will enable you to compare how well each person has met the key performance factors (SKAMPEs) needed to be effective in the position.

If you are accepting CVs, a well–constructed CV will be short and concise, well presented and organised. Remember that CVs can be written to impress. Look out for:

❑ Gaps and inconsistencies in timing.
❑ Verifiable qualifications.
❑ Several jobs in the last two or three years.
❑ Illogical career moves in the past.
❑ Extreme high and low earnings.
❑ Salary progression.
❑ Vague reasons for leaving.
❑ Missing references.
❑ Is the candidate making a logical move this time?

Before assessing each applicant's suitability for the role, we suggest you generate an Applicant Tracking Form for each application as this will help you keep score.

This systematic approach ensures that:

❏ Each applicant is measured against the same criteria.

❏ Applicants are compared to each other objectively and systematically.

❏ You focus on those SKAMPEs that are essential for high performance.

❏ You avoid focusing on irrelevant factors.

Because you may not collect information on a person for one purpose and then use it for another, it is important to ask unsuccessful applicants whether they want their application returned to them or whether it can be destroyed or kept on file for future positions.

Applicant tracking form

On the facing page is a form designed to track job applicants. It provides a simple method for scoring them.

There are many elements that affect job performance. Each of these must be considered when making the hiring decision. The following format will help you evaluate each candidate against an effective range of criteria.

Rate each candidate on each of these elements by placing a checkmark in the appropriate box.

Then complete the simple calculations to generate a Relative Composite Rating for the candidate.

Applicant tracking form

	Not at all what job requires	Less than job requires	Adequate for the job	More than the job requires	Far more than job requires
Application form					
Education/Qualifications					
Job–related experience					
General employment requirements					
Telephone screen					
Psychometric Assessment					
Reference check					
Main interview					
Personal presentation					
Total marks					
	x1	x2	x3	x4	x5
Multiply by weighting					

Relative Composite Rating: add the scores in the line above, and place the final rating here.

Application forms

Employers should be encouraged to use application forms especially for mid to lower level positions within the organisation. Application forms will collect the information you want. CVs only contains the information the candidate wants to give you!

Here are some idea starters for your application form. Besides the normal biographical information, work history and reference points, think of other 'must haves' for the position. You may want to cover such things as:

Hours of work — 'Our business runs 24/7. Can you work shifts at any time?'

Or 'Sometime we may need extra hands to work after hours with little notice. Would that be a problem?'

Medical — 'Can you lift heavy weights/packages etc? Do you have a medical condition that prevents heavy lifting?'

Or 'We have stringent hygiene regulations; do you have any known health problems which will prevent you from doing this job? Are you prepared to undergo a medical examination at our cost?'

Or, 'Smoking is only allowed within designated breaks and in designated places. Would this be a problem for you? (Being a smoker cannot be used as a reason to not employ — however all New Zealand workplaces are now smoke free by law).

Criminal — 'Do you have any charges pending?' Or 'Have you had any criminal convictions in the last five years? If so please detail these.' Check this question out with the 'clean slate' law.

Immigration — 'Do you have a legal right to work in New Zealand? If yes, 'By what means?'

The above are thought starters. You may have a number of other questions that will serve as an immediate screening–out alert, for example, a current first–aid certificate for home care positions.

Remember, you cannot ask questions that do not directly relate to the person being able to do the job (refer back to questions you can/cannot ask on pages 56—61).

Finally, any deliberate untruths on the application form by the employee, which are uncovered later, may justify dismissal — but you must state this fact in the application form. To this end we recommend all application forms are signed as read and understood and attached to the employee's personal file.

The following pages demonstrate some of the key elements of a good application form:

Application for employment
Personal details

Position applied for	
Surname	
First names	
Current address	
	Post code
Telephone	*Home:* *Mob:*
Email address	

Application for employment
Education Details

(Includes tertiary and further education establishments)

School/college/ tech/university	
Dates	From: To:
Standards attained/ qualifications	
School/college/ tech/university	
Dates	From: To:
Standards attained/ qualifications	

Other qualifications/skills that may benefit this position

Qualification/skill	
Date and place achieved	
Qualification/skill	
Date and place achieved	

Application for employment
Employment History

(Please list from most recent/present employer first)

Employer	
Address	
Dates	From: To:
Position held	
Main duties and responsibilities	
Reason for leaving	
Rate of pay	

Employer	
Address	
Dates	From: To:
Position held	
Main duties and responsibilities	
Reason for leaving	
Rate of pay	

Application for employment
Referees
Please provide latest employer and at least one previous employer

Name	
Title	
Relationship to applicant	
Telephone	Bus: Mob:

Name	
Title	
Relationship to applicant	
Telephone	Bus: Mob:

Name	
Title	
Relationship to applicant	
Telephone	Bus: Mob:

Application for employment

General information

Are you a New Zealand citizen?	Yes	No
If no, do you have the right to work in New Zealand?	Yes	No
Do you have a work permit?	Yes	No
If yes, when does this expire?		
Have you ever been convicted of a criminal offence?	Yes	No
If so, give brief details.		
Have you ever been arrested or tried for a criminal offence, had a criminal conviction, or are you currently before the court or awaiting a hearing or outcome (Clean Slate Act applies)?	Yes	No
If so, give brief details.		
Have you ever been dismissed from any previous employment?	Yes	No
If so, give brief details.		
Have you ever been the subject of an accusation and /or investigation for dishonesty by a previous employer?	Yes	No
If so, give brief details.		
How many days have you missed from work/school over the past year other than approved holiday/sick/ disabiltiy leave?		

Application for employment
General information

How many days have you been late to work/school over the past year other than approved holiday/sick/ disabiltiy leave?		

What class of driving licence do you have? (If relevant to job)		

Do you have any demerit points? If so, how many? (If relevant to job)		

Do you know any person currently employed by this company?	Yes	No

If so, give brief details.	

Are you prepared to work overtime?	Yes	No

Do you have secondary employment?	Yes	No

If so, give brief details.	

If you are offered a position, when is the earliest you could commence?	

What is the minimum salary you will accept?	

What transportation arrangements do you have to attend your place of work?	

Other interests — please list any hobbies/sporting interests:

Application for employment
Medical information

Have you ever suffered from an injury at work that required you to take time off?	Yes No
If so, give brief details.	
Do you have any illness or injury that might prevent you from performing your work?	Yes No
If so, give brief details.	
Are there any special services or facilities we need to provide to enable you to carry out the work duties?	Yes No
If so, give brief details.	
Have you ever taken more than 5 days absence due to your own illness in the last 12 months?	Yes No
Do you smoke?	Yes No

Checking against performance factors

While screening applicants, you have the ideal opportunity to begin matching their perceptions of their own skills and abilities with the main performance factors you have identified for this job.

Using the top eight factors identified in the Job Analysis Survey (see page 33), you can create a form for applicants to fill in at an early stage of the recruitment process.

Here's an example of how the form could look:

The Performance Factors

On a rating scale of 1 to 5 (where 5=excellent and 1=not of interest, or may need training), rate yourself against the following performance factors needed for this job:

Rating

1. *List your top–ranked performance factor here*

2. *List your second highest–ranked performance factor here, and so on . . .*

3.

4.

5.

6.

7.

8.

Competitive Advantage

Briefly outline why you would be the best person for this position:

Reducing the risks

By asking the applicant to make a formal declaration about their job application, you'll reduce the risks of abuse or at the very least provide evidence which can be used later in the event of any misuse of the application process.

Here's a sample declaration to accompany the application form:

Declaration

I declare that the information provided in my Job Application Form is to the best of my knowledge a true and correct record. I consent to the company seeking verbal or written information on a confidential basis about me, from representatives of my previous employers and/or referees, and I authorise the information sought to be used by the company for the purpose of ascertaining my suitability for the position for which I am applying.

I authorize this company, if applicable, to request a copy of my credit and qualifications record, motor vehicle driving record, and any other investigative report deemed necessary through various third party sources. I will be notified as to the nature and scope of such investigations. I hereby agree if required, to submit to any drug/alcohol test required of me. I understand that the information received by the company is supplied in confidence as evaluative material and will not be disclosed to me.

Have you read the Job Position Description? | Yes | | No |

_____   _____

Applicant's signature   *Date*

Checking the contents of the application form

We are still in the selecting–out stage. Those applicants who meet the initial requirements (have the Knowledge, Skill and Experience) for the role can now be interviewed. This is not a full behavioural–based interview. It is more a 'checking procedure'. You are validating the information you have from the application form, covering any gaps and testing oral communication — can they speak English?

There are two ways to conduct initial screen outs — via the telephone and face to face. Once again this depends on the number of applicants and the type of job. Telephone interviewing is ideal for jobs that require little customer or personal interaction. However, for roles like retail sales, you may want to assess personal appearance quickly, so face–to–face interviews are best.

You are still in the pre–screen process and are probably dealing with a number of applicants, so it's important to keep a tight time frame on this part of the process. Keep the pre–screen interviews brief — 15 to 20 minutes should suffice.

Suggested preliminary telephone questions:

Firstly, you need to address and clarify any concerns on the application form.

Following this, settle on three of four questions that indicate whether the candidate meets your minimum hiring requirements. If you find they don't, there's no reason to take them to the next step, psychometric testing, and the main interview.

People who need a job will tell you what you want to hear. You need to drill down quickly on the non–negotiable areas — hours of work are always a priority for entry work positions.

Prospective employees will tell they are prepared to work any days, hours, or times you want. However, if hired and the hours are not to their liking, they'll soon be showing up late or not at all.

Head off this aggravation up front by asking these questions before the applicant knows what days/hours/shifts you need to fill:

❏ What days/hours/shifts do you prefer not to work?

❏ What days/hours/shifts can you work?

❏ What days/hours/shifts can't you work or don't want to work?

Will the applicant be happy working for what you're paying or will this be a stop–gap position to a better–paying job? Ask about . . .

❏ What is your minimum salary expectation?

❏ Can they start the job when needed and be there on time each day?

❏ If hired, when are you available to start?

❏ Do you have reliable transportation?

❏ At your last job, what was the latest you ever arrived at work?

Past behavior is our best indicator of future behavior. Ask:

❏ What's the hardest job you've ever had and how long were you there?

❏ Have you ever been fired or asked to resign from a job? Explain.

❏ Tell me about the times you've been given added responsibilities, a promotion, or raise.

❏ What did/do you like about your last/current job?

❏ What attracts you to our company and this job?

You will also be assessing oral communication. In some positions this telephone interview will serve as a work sample test. For example, if the role is for a receptionist, customer service or call centre, how is this person presenting?

Are they polite? Communicative? Do they sound service orientated?

Note: There have been a number of new developments in the screening–out process. Once you have screened down from the application form and telephone interview, you can use a pre–screening employment test to check the roots of the tree. This will save a huge amount of management time as you will have all the information you need to reject candidates without embarking on expensive and time–consuming interviews.

More details on pre–screening employment tests are in the next chapter.

Telephone screening

The telephone is a wonderful tool to help screen applicants, providing you ask the right questions and follow a well–prepared interview structure.

Once you've made contact, set the scene with something like:

'Of the many applications we have received we would like to take yours to the next stage. Do you have about 15 minutes to talk now, or shall I call back at a more convenient time? I'd like to ask some questions, but first let me quickly explain this position.'

(Give a brief job description, pay and benefits, hours of work etc. Then ask if they are still interested in proceeding).

If they want to proceed, here are some questions designed to elicit important information at an early stage:

INITIAL SCREENING

Question 1: *'Tell me about your last job? What aspects did you like most? Why? Also, which did you like least? Why?'*

Listen and probe for milestones, accomplishments, relations with work supervisors and co–workers, tasks liked/disliked, reason for leaving jobs, etc. Probe how prior experience has prepared him/her for this job.

Question 2: *'Why are you considering leaving, or why did you leave your current/last job?'*

Listen for reliability and job fit.

Question 3: *'What attracts you to this job at our company?'*

Listen for a desire to work and a desire to serve others as well as an interest in your organisation.

Question 4: *'What hours are you willing to work? Which hours do you prefer to work?'*

Does this suit the hours required of the present position?

Question 5: *'What is your salary expectation and how do you see this structured?'*

'Must haves': Double check/probe to ensure the candidate has the specific knowledge/skill that you identified for this role through the Job Analysis Survey (page 33) for this role (such as being able to use your software, basic accounting functions, certificates, qualifications etc).

Oral communication: Listen for social skills, friendliness, clear concise speech, and enthusiasm — evidence that they are self–driven.

Make an assessment as to whether the candidate meets the requirements of the position. If they do, invite the candidate to complete 'our job–fit assessment' on site at a suitable time.

Remember to record your assessment of the candidate in the Applicant Tracking Form (see page 65).

Step Three Reminders . . .

— Is your approach to screen out or screen in?
— Review the application form. Screen out all people who do not have the knowledge, skill and experience for the role.
— Screen the remainder via telephone interview. Validate the information given to you on the application form and challenge any gaps. Also assess oral communication.
— Make sure you have given a realistic job preview up front. Do this with the application form and reiterate in the telephone interview.
— Arrange an appointment to do an employment test — check out the roots!
Note: You can automate most of the recruitment process using the AssessSystems online Applicant Processing System.

6. EMPLOYEE PROFILING

Step 4: Identifying the 'real' person before you hire

Why consider using any form of psychometric test when hiring or developing employees? Mike Smith, in his excellent book, *Testing People at Work*, explains it succinctly . . .

'People are different. Some are intelligent, whilst others are slow witted. Some are warm hearted, whilst others are cold blooded. Some are motivated by money, whilst others are motivated by ideas. Jobs differ too. Some require slow—witted, cold—blooded people who are motivated by money.

'The task is to measure people's characteristics in some way, so that these characteristics can be matched to the requirements of the job.'

The only way to accomplish this is through psychometric testing. Yes, I can hear you now — 'Psychometric testing, what is all this mind—reading mumbo jumbo about?'

One of the first things I learnt, and found difficult to do, was to throw out the academic language. Managers (and candidates) find the word 'psych' and 'test' complicated and frightening. One client said it seemed to explain a medical procedure for brain scanning! These are not 'tests'. A test implies 'pass or fail' and it's not about that — it's about 'job fit'. There is a job for everyone. Our task is to ensure the person we hire fits our job, so both the candidate and the organisation benefits.

So when referring to this process in the workplace let's get rid of any implied medical connotations — it's out with 'psychological' and 'test' and in with 'Job Fit Survey', Employee Assessment' or 'Employee Profiling'. I think these are more commercially acceptable and induce less confusion and nervousness.

I should note that it is correct to refer to mental ability or cognitive assessments as 'tests'. The questions asked do have a 'right or wrong' answer. But my overall point is to de–emphasise the need to 'pass' to get the job.

Where does employee profiling fit into the selection process?

In Chapter 1 we used the tree analogy to explain the hiring process.

To refresh, the fruits on a tree help explain what a person can do. As this part of the tree is above ground, the fruit of the tree can be seen; this is represented by the candidate's job Knowledge, Technical Skills and Experience required for the specific job role you are assessing. These job specifications (as opposed to person specifications) are observable and trainable.

Employee profiling is the only way to check out the roots of the tree. Here we are assessing who the person is. Will they be able to do the job, and how well? *Can* the person do the job and *how* they will do the job are two very different things. Managers are very competent at assessing the *can*, but they rely on emotion, personal impressions, and gut feel to judge *how* the candidate will perform.

By using employee profiling, we take a scientific approach

to understanding the innate personal characteristics, mental abilities and attitudes of a prospective employee. These characteristics cannot be observed or assessed during the selection process, in an interview, or via the reports from given referees. They can only be measured through a validated and reliable employment profile.

When it comes to the roots of the tree, too many managers rely on their own impressions. You cannot 'read' people in a one–hour interview.

A person who presents well and communicates effectively at interview may not perform satisfactorily on the job. Remember, the person you see at interview will be as well presented as you will ever see them!

Most managers' make hiring decisions based on what a person *can* do, but will always have problems or terminations based on *who they are*!

Job Fit Surveys, or Employee Profiles are best for assessing the less obvious personal attributes and abilities required for any job. Many hiring managers think the use of these tools are extremely expensive and time consuming and therefore should only be used for top management positions. Nothing could be further from the truth.

It's important to make the right hiring decisions, whether we are employing a warehouse worker or a chief financial officer. Understanding the candidates 'roots' will go a long way in achieving that, irrespective of the job role.

Benchmarking

Testing individuals and understanding their 'roots' will serve to tell us what type of person they are. However, this is only half the story.

We need to know if that person's innate capabilities will 'fit' the job.

Employee profiling becomes more powerful when we can benchmark the results to a specific job position. This is referred to as 'criterion–related validity.' For example we can test all current employees and correlate their scores against an objective measure of performance.

This is usually an expensive and time–consuming exercise. However, the Prevue Assessment platform has managed to replicate this process with their Job Description Survey. Several people who understand the requirements to be successful in the role complete the Job Description Survey.

This survey contains a number of job behaviours. Respondents are asked to indicate the importance of each behaviour as it relates to job success.

The Prevue system then collates these results and produces a Benchmark Report. Raters can then discuss difference and agree on the final benchmark that is then activated in the system. Applicants' scores are then overlaid to this benchmark and a cut–off score is produced.

These benchmarks can be produced quickly and inexpensively, creating a profile that describes whether the applicant is the right fit for the role.

Before discussing the types of employment tests that are available I want to stress that test results are very good at showing you the 'red flags' but not necessarily good at identifying the 'stars'.

In fact I tend to get more suspicious when I see an extremely 'strong' profile.

Usually these profile results come with a 'positive response' warning; more on this subject shortly.

Types of employment tests

There are seven main types of employment tests:

☐ Mental abilities tests.

☐ Personality tests.

☐ Attitudes tests (integrity).

☐ Interests and motivations.

☐ Sales tests.

☐ Teamwork and communication styles.

☐ Skills testing.

Note: The job interview is also a 'test'. However, in most cases it has no scientific basis and lacks standardisation. In fact, the way most interviews are conducted, an unstructured chit chat makes them the least valid and most expensive selection tool to use — expensive in management time and in the risk of hiring the wrong person. For more information, visit the articles library at our website.

Mental ability tests

Years of research have shown that a person's mental abilities give a good indication of the person's likely success on the job. In fact, they are the highest predictors of job performance. There are many mental ability tests, some of which indicate overall intellectual ability, others to indicate a specific ability e.g. numerical reasoning ability, or mechanical reasoning.

These tests are always timed, are on–line or pencil–and–paper based and vary in length from 5 to 20 minutes.

Here are a few examples of specific abilities that can be assessed:

☐ Critical reasoning — measures high level verbal and numerical reasoning ability.

❐ Abstract reasoning — measures ability to analyse logical relationships and discover principles underlying those relationships.

❐ Verbal reasoning and comprehension — measures ability to analyse information and make valid judgments about that information, and the ability to understand the usage and meaning of the written and spoken word.

❐ Numerical reasoning and ability — measures the ability to perceive and understand the relationships in a series of figures and use basic mathematical skills.

❐ Visual speed and accuracy — measures ability to see details quickly and accurately. Ideal for people filling warehouse orders.

❐ Manual speed and accuracy — measures ability to make fine finger movements rapidly and accurately.

Tests of mental ability are relevant for most jobs because intelligence determines the rate at which people process information. Time taken to process information controls the rate at which people learn on the job (training) and the ability to cope with the novel aspects of the job (Smith, 2005).

These types of tests are sometimes labeled as cognitive tests and they are usually divided into two areas — ability and aptitude tests. An abilities test usually measures the person's broad talent applying to a wide range of tasks. These tests mainly measure verbal, numerical and spatial ability in a single time test.

Aptitude tests are generally narrower and apply to the way in which an actual skill is used. Examples of aptitude testing would be mechanical reasoning and visual speed (ideal for people that have to match order numbers on documents with product on the shelves). At AssessSystems we have several mental ability tests: some of these are combined with personality measurements; others are stand alone. Time factors vary from 8 minutes through to 20 minutes and costs for one–off bureau testing can range from $25 to $50.

Personality profiling

Personality profiles can be used to assess a wide range of personality attributes — anywhere between 5 and 30. To be legally defensible the personality attributes assessed must be relevant to success on the job — 'job fit'.

Personality profiles explain the style of how things will be done — the person's innate characteristics, of their preferred way of doing things or reacting. For example, will a person be impulsive, persuasive and resilient? Or will they be cautious, accommodating and anxious?

Science now states that the development of personality is driven 50% by genetics and 50% by environment in early years of life. By the time we're into our late teens our personality is cemented. There is evidence from the 30–year study conducted by the University of Otago Medical School on twins that the child you see at three will be the adult you see at 30!

Yes, we can change our personality in certain situations. But we always go back to home base. Imagine if you hired a salesperson that lacked 'sales personality' — low optimism, no resilience or assertiveness, no motivation to influence and persuade. No amount of training will turn this person into a successful salesperson. They are simply in the wrong profession.

It's accepted that the taxonomy (the systematic structure) of personality is now based on the Big Five:

Conscientiousness: The degree to which an individual is persistent, motivated, and organised; ranging from highly disciplined and dependable to lackadaisical and carefree.

Likeability: The degree to which the individual is pleasant and agreeable; ranging from warm, tolerant and tactful to tough minded, sceptical and direct.

Unconventional: The degree to which the individual is predictable, rules oriented and structured, or is open to new ideas and is adventuresome and possibly inconsistent.

Extroversion: The style and focus of an individual's emotional energy; ranging from outgoing, dominant, ambitious, and sociable to introverted, shy and quiet.

Stability: The degree to which an individual is emotionally sound and resistant to stress.

A good way to remember this is with the acronym CLUES —see our popular pre–screening assessment PeopleCLUES.

It is accepted by personnel psychologists that our innate characteristics can be explained by examining 30 personality traits. We don't need to measure all 30 of these to get an understanding of job fit. We can decide the type of personality assessment to use depending on the role and whether we are selecting in or selecting out.

Personality assessments (along with other assessments, like mental ability and attitudes) can be used early in the selection process to screen out unsuitable applicants (PeopleCLUES is a good example), or used later to screen in suitable applicants (ASSESS and Prevue are a good examples). For more information, go to www.assess.co.nz.

The type of assessment will vary depending on the stage in the selection process at which the test is employed. When there are large numbers of applicants it is advisable to screen out early on the key personality attributes required for success in the position. These pre–screening tests e.g. PeopleCLUES are lower in cost, easy to administer, require no expert interpretation, suit lower level roles and are predictive of work attitude but not necessarily of work performance.

If the test is placed later in the selection it is used to gather in–depth insights on the short–listed applicants for comparative purposes. Here we are selecting prime candidates. These tests are highly predictive of job performance because they are benchmarked against specific job competencies. They tend to be more expensive, but provide a deeper interpretation.

Commonly assessed personality attributes are:

❏ Independent versus diplomatic.

❏ Conscientious versus spontaneous.

❏ Extroverted versus introverted.

❏ Open versus conventional.

❏ Stable versus emotional.

Better personality assessments, like our premier instrument for the selection and development of managerial and professional positions (it's called ASSESS), combine various personality characteristics to provide an accurate picture of more complex performance factors and competencies including:

❏ Communication skills.

❏ Customer service focus.

❏ Initiative.

❏ Innovation.

❏ Stress tolerance.

❏ Teamwork.

❏ Leadership.

❏ Managing others.

❏ Planning/organising.

❏ Sales ability.

❏ Negotiating ability.

❑ Building relationships.

The AssessSystems range of personality and mental ability assessments can be benchmarked against specific positions such as those in:

❑ Reception.

❑ Administrative/clerical.

❑ Customer service.

❑ Hospitality.

❑ Production and distribution.

❑ Retail sales/management.

❑ Sales.

❑ Health care.

❑ Call centres, help desks.

❑ Drivers.

❑ Supermarket checkout.

❑ Personal services.

❑ Professional positions.

❑ Managers.

The personality attributes for each of these positions have been found to predict job effectiveness in that position. For example, the personality attributes predictive of success in a retail management position are:

❑ Positive sales attitude — attitude about the customer and sales.

❑ Leadership — inclination to lead others.

❑ Persuasiveness — ability to influence customers.

❑ Energy — activity level and ability to take action.

❑ Good judgement — tendency to think objectively.

❑ Organisation and attention to detail — approach to structuring the workload successfully and attention to detail.

❑ Frustration tolerance — ability to remain emotionally positive despite problems and set–backs. Personality assessments can take anywhere between 15 and 50 minutes to complete and can cost between $50 and $350. The personality assessments we use at AssessSystems can also have mental ability testing built in. A mental abilities test is always strongly recommended irrespective of the position.

Attitude assessments

Attitude assessments usually fall under the general heading of integrity assessments, or assessments of counter–productive behaviours. Values usually drive attitudes, and attitudes are reflected in behaviour. Adding this form of assessment into the first part of your 'screening out' process for entry–level positions can save large amounts of management time. The PeopleCLUES suite of assessments includes an excellent attitudes assessment. It highlights six areas of counter–productive behaviours. These are:

Honesty: Will they steal from you?

Drugs and alcohol: The effects may impact on honesty (above) and conscientiousness (below).

Conscientiousness: Will they show up for work on time and be reliable?

Computer abuse: Will they use company time and internet facilities for personal use?

Aggression: Will they upset others with intimidating behaviour or, at worst, punch somebody's lights out?

Sexual harrassment: Self explanatory.

Sexual harrassment

This takes 15 to 20 minutes to complete and can be used as a stand–alone measure. It is used in conjunction with personality or mental ability as a block of tests. This format is ideal for pre–

screening large numbers of applicants.

Interest and motivations

Motivation is a major factor in job performance. An employee may have excellent personality but produce nothing unless motivated. Smith (2005) expresses the following hypothetical formula:

Job Performance = mental ability + personality x motivation

Measures of job interest and motivation are used extensively in career–guidance work. They can become very useful in specific job roles; is a salesperson motivated by money, contact with people, learning and explaining new technology? The AssessSystems product — Prevue, includes an interest/motivation measure that also covers mental ability and personality. This is an excellent all–round assessment for all job roles. Our SalesMax assessment (for sales selection and development) also tests for sales motivations.

Sales assessments

These are specifically designed for the selection of salespeople and usually include personality, sales knowledge and sales motivation. One such tool is SalesMax (See web link in the appendix for more information). At AssessSystems we have had great success over the last 10 years predicting successful sales people using this assessment. SalesMax measures sales personality, sales knowledge and sales motivation. Having the right sales personality is key to sales success. If your candidate lacks resilience, motivation to persuade, willingness to confront, listening ability, assertiveness, energy etc. no amount of sales training will improve performance. The person is in the wrong profession — there is no JOB FIT.

Teamwork and communication

These tools are usually focused on four or five dimensions. Many of these tools are inexpensive. Some are free. Many are unreliable. Most common are DISC and Myers Briggs. They measure observed behaviour — how we respond to the four Ps of performance: problems, people, place, and procedures. Although important, the four Ps do not tell us *why*.

My colleague Ira Wolf, of Success Performance Solutions, uses a motoring analogy to explain the difference between these behavioural instruments and a personality assessment.

Using a behavioural instrument like DISC or Myers Briggs to understand future on–the–job performance will help you identify the colour, make and model of the car, but will tell you nothing about the engine — what's under the bonnet. This is driven by a person's innate personality characteristics.

Too many managers hire on imprecise observations and then have painfully learned that what you see is not always what you get. This is akin to purchasing a car with the bonnet welded shut! At AssessSystems, our tool of preference in this area is MyHardwired. This instrument measures not only preferred and expected style but also intrinsic style and therein lies the difference against any DISC or Myers Briggs product.

These behavioural instruments are ideal for identifying group styles to enhance communication and team building.

In short, these behavioural tools should never be used for selecting employees, because they cannot be measured against specific job roles and/or individuals and so they cannot be used to predict future performance or compare one person against another.

Take it as a 'given' from the psychological community that ipsative tools like these, used on their own, are not valid predictors of work performance — the Myers Briggs website alerts users to this fact.

Drug testing

This is becoming more common and some major organisations have introduced drug testing into their test battery, particularly if the job role involves a high degree of safety. These physical tests are quick and non–evasive and are conducted by specialist testing agencies. However, abstinence and masking agents can make this procedure unreliable — dare I mention Tour de France!

As outlined in the section on Attitude Tests, the CLUES Attitude test will measure 'admissions' and/or acceptance to drug usage. This type of counter–productive behaviour test endeavours to uncover a candidate's attitudes to drugs or alcohol use/abuse. The theory is that a positive, accepting attitude will most likely be reflected in behaviour.

In summary, the use of employment assessments provides an objective, unbiased assessment of personality attributes, mental abilities, motivation, interests and attitudes. These personal attributes and abilities have been found to be a good indicator of likely performance in a variety of positions, especially if you have benchmarked these against the requirements to be successful in the position. These personal characteristics also provide insights that show where further investigating or checking should be done. Most assessment reports provide interview questions and reference probes for this purpose.

Skills testing

Although not a strict psychometric test, using skills tests during your pre–employment screening process will also help you evaluate a candidate's readiness for the job. Our skills tests are developed by Subject Matter Experts (SME's) and help identify a candidate's strengths and weaknesses in relation to key knowledge and skills areas. It helps take the guesswork out of hiring by helping ensure that a candidate's knowledge and skills in relation to the role (say, being able to confidently use Microsoft Excel) match what is listed on their application form or CV. AssessSystems' skills tests are also used to measure incumbent's knowledge and skills in order to support career development and training initiatives. Our skills testing application is one of the only products that provides authoring tools that allow you to create your own tests for training and employee–development purposes.

AssessSystems offers an extensive test catalogue with hundreds of skills assessment tests in categories such as: Accounting/Financial, Call Center, Clerical, Microsoft Office, Engineering, Industrial / Warehouse, Medical, Retail, Banking.

Validity and reliability of assessments

There are many good books available on this subject. However, it is important to have a basic understanding to help you evaluate what tools to use and, more importantly, what tools not to use.

Validity

Validity refers to what characteristics the test measures and how accurately the test measures that characteristic. The lay definition of validity is 'the extent to which a score measures what it purports to measure'. A more academic definition is, 'best available approximation to the truth or falsity of a given inference, proposition or conclusion' (Cook and Campbell, 1979).

Validity is about the strength of our conclusions, inferences or propositions. In short, were we right? Validity tells you if the characteristic being measured by a test is related to job qualifications and requirements. Validity evidence indicates that there is linkage between test performance and job performance.

Validity also describes the extent to which you could make specific conclusions or predictions about people based on their test scores. It indicates the usefulness of the test. It is important to understand the difference between reliability and validity.

Validity will tell you how good a test is for a particular situation; reliability will tell you how trustworthy a score on the test will be. You cannot draw valid conclusions from a test score unless you are sure that the test is reliable. Even when a test is reliable, it may not be valid. Be careful that any test you select is both reliable and valid for your situation.

A test's validity is established in reference to a specific purpose. The test may not be valid for different purposes. For example, a test used to make valid predictions about somebody's technical proficiency on the job may not be valid for predicting his or her leadership skills.

Criteria or predictive validity

We touched on this earlier when discussing benchmarking. Criteria or predictive validity is a statistical review that demonstrates a relationship between an assessment and measures of job performance.

A sales organisation may use an assessment (the predictor) to assess the sales capability of a job candidate (criteria). We would first want to assess all current sales people and grade these people on specific performance criteria: revenue written each month (objective) or client–service ability (subjective).

Our statistician would then look for assessment scores that identify the good and the poor performers. We could then use these results to predict future performance and thus agree that the assessment used measured what it purports to measure — sales success, and so is valid. This is often referred to as 'benchmarking' and can be done inexpensively and quickly using either CLUES and/or PREVUE assessments.

Reliability

Reliability is about consistency. If I was to assess you today and then re–assess you in six months time, I would want minimal variance in the result.

Statisticians define reliability as the proportion of variance that is not due to random error. Error can be large or small. This may occur for numerous reasons. We may have assessed the person in a very calm, quiet environment. The second application of the assessment may have been done in a very noisy, hot environment. The results would not be reliable. Errors in the design of the assessment itself would also make it unreliable.

The validity of common hiring tools

The numbers in this section represent the predictive validity of each process. In the table overleaf, the validity rating of 0.14, for instance, tells us that when using an unstructured interview, we have no better than around a one–in–six chance of getting it right. As you can see from our list, mental ability testing is the most powerful single predictor of job performance, irrespective of the role. However, it is still no better than the toss of a coin. This is why a combination of selection methods is used.

Unstructured interview: score 0.14
❏ A general discussion between manager and candidate.
❏ Questions are unprepared and not rated.

Reference checking: score 0.26
❏ From a structured reference checking form.

Biodata form: score 0.30
❏ Rating the candidate's suitability from a range of personal data collected through a carefully structured Application Form.

Personality profile: score 0.38
❏ A validated test that measures the candidate's 'personality traits' like assertiveness, aggression, sociability — BUT not benched marked to the specific job role.

Structured interview: score 0.46
❏ A multi–rated structured interview using behavioural–based interview questions.

Mental abilities test: score 0.54
❏ Examples are tests that measure the candidate's numerical, verbal, mechanical, dexterity skills etc.

Interest Test: score 0.66
❏ Usually based on the candidate's interest in working with data, things, people and ideas. If the candidate's interests are correlated with the job tasks, this leads to more motivation and hence better job performance.

Job matching (benchmarked): score 0.75
❏ Using a combination of the above measures, ensuring the employment tests are specifically benchmarked to the role.

High turnover industry

Were the candidates job–matched?	No	Yes
% who quit or were dismissed after 6 months	46%	24%
% who quit or were dismissed after 14 months	57%	28%

Sample size = 13,102. Source: Greenberg & Greenberg (1985)

Low turnover industry

Were the candidates job–matched?	No	Yes
% who quit or were dismissed after 6 months	25%	5%
% who quit or were dismissed after 14 months	34%	8%

Sample size = 5,941. Source: Greenberg & Greenberg (1985)

As the above tables demonstrate, an employment test for personality and mental ability coupled with a structured, multi–rated interview, both aligned (benchmarked against the job), provides a very strong selection process.

This combination gave a 50% reduction in turnover in high turnover industries and a 500% turnover reduction in low turnover industries.

But what about faking?

Mental ability tests are reliable because faking is not a problem. Who would want to purposely give incorrect answers to a test of mental ability? The situation is different when measuring personality, motives, interests and attitudes. Candidates naturally see these assessments as being 'tests' that they must 'pass' in order to be successful in gaining employment. Therefore it is in their interest to try and answer questions in a manner that will achieve this objective.

The trouble with faking is that it is not a constant. Some people may not fake at all, some may fake a little, others a little more and a few fake a lot. To overcome this situation, and/or detect faking, personnel psychologists construct questions, methods of answering, frame initial test instructions and build in specific triggers to detect degrees of faking.

There has been a tremendous amount of work done over the last 10 years in terms of test faking in respect to job performance. Psychologists Mount and Barrack (1995) have done considerable work in this area. The consensus is that if a person has the ability to manage their self–impression during a personality assessment then they have the same ability to do that at the coal face. At the end of the day, is there anything wrong with that? In fact it may be said it could be a measure of success for a sales position. Conversely, it could be a red flag if the assessment was for a financial position.

This highlights the best way to interpret assessment results. Candidates will rarely fake bad and faking good is usually detected, or shown, by overly 'perfect' results. For this reason, assessments are highly reliable for showing us individuals with poor job fit as opposed to those that will be the 'superstars'.

Combining the insights
Once an assessment has highlighted the personality attributes, mental abilities or attitudes that show potential

concerns, these have to be explored further. This can be done through the interview (the benefit of doing a pre–screen test) and through reference checking. All employment tests used by AssessSystems provide you with a set of behavioural interview questions, as well as a set of reference–checking questions.

If an applicant for the retail manager position has been assessed as having low frustration tolerance, a possible follow–up interview question could be:

'Describe those aspects of your previous jobs which have frustrated or irritated you.'

The interviewer would then listen for responses that confirm a low–frustration tolerance, or a tendency to be easily disappointed or upset.

Seeking verbal feedback

Psychometric test results are reported against specific populations and/or job roles. These results, usually from a large population sample, produce a bell curve. The bell curve is divided into ten equally wide dimensions called standard tenths or stens. Approximately 16% of the population will have sten scores in the 1–3 range, 16% will score in the 8–10 range and the remaining 68% will score in the middle range of 4–7. When interpreting a candidate's results, you can be very confident that scores which fall in the lower left or right of the curve are the ones that wave the 'red or green flags.' To help with test interpretation we strongly recommend you seek verbal feedback from a certified assessment interpreter.

Verbal feedback adds power to the selection evaluation process and should always support the written report. Never take the written report as a 'given'. At AssessSystems we strongly encourage hiring managers to discuss the report contents, especially if the testing was done on one or two final candidates — selecting in. Giving verbal feedback to clients gives us a chance to play 'devil's advocate.'

Usually at this stage of the hiring process the manager has made up her mind based on emotion and gut feel. If the assessment counteracts this 'feeling' the manager will tend to ignore the negatives, seeing them as something they can manage around, or train for.

This rarely happens! Verbal feedback is often more powerful than any written report. Use it!

Work–sample testing

Requiring a prospective employee to complete mini tasks is a good predictor of future performance on the job. A work sample is not suitable for all positions but, where they can be created, it is advisable to do so.

Position	Work sample
Bartender	Mixing drinks
Sales represenative	A sales presentation
Receptionist	Answering a few calls
Receptionist	Dealing with a difficult client

Work samples can provide an accurate and consistent measure of performance factors required for success. The initial telephone interview can serve as a mini work–sample test.

If the job is for a call centre, receptionist, customer–service position, do this candidate's oral communication skills measure up? If it is a sales role, are they selling you?

Using assessments for employee development

Training new employees can be a costly exercise. Identifying what training is needed is an important starting point. Many times this is accomplished through general observation, or requests from employees. Employers often take a blanket approach to training. They fail to identify individual needs and align training to these needs appropriately. The latter is much more effective and much less costly.

Employee assessments are also ideal for identifying individual training needs of incumbents in relationship to specific job–performance factors. This should not be confused with skills training. Assessments that measure and report results based on specific performance factors (job competencies), such as the ASSESS development and ASSESS 360 Feedback Reports are ideal. They can pinpoint employee weaknesses and align these with training needs.

The ASSESS Development report will highlight *why* an employee performs in a specific way and the ASSESS 360 Report will show *how* they are doing their core task. Combining these results gives a very powerful employee development platform.

Summary

The evidence from decades of psychological study confirms that the use of a valid and reliable tool to assess a candidate's personality, mental ability and attitudes in relation to the job they are applying for (job fit) will dramatically improve your chance of avoiding hiring the wrong person.

There are thousands of assessments available on the market. No one assessment will be appropriate for every job role, unless it is very expensive. That does not make budgetary sense. It is strongly recommended that when seeking advice or using psychological assessments, you rely on trained personnel who have in–field experience to enable you to make sound judgement calls — an organisational psychologist.

There are many 'salespeople' pushing assessments that may look wonderful and indeed produce results that 'paint an observable picture' after a test trial. Many of these are unreliable because they are inappropriate to the situation. In many cases the assessments peddled by untrained people lack any form of validity or reliability. It is not that they intend to deceive buy they lack the scientific training and background in organisational psychology to understand what constitutes an appropriate tool for the specific situation.

'It is proven that employee testing dramatically improves your selection process and ensures you don't hire a horror story. Employee testing helps you to economically select out those candidates that do not 'fit' the role and if hired will not perform, impacting directly and indirectly on your business. It's estimated that 80% of a manager's 'people time' is spent on poor performers.'

Step Four Reminders . . .

— Always use, at least, a personality and mental ability assessment. Don't rely on your gut feel to understand the 'roots of the tree'.

— Assessments of personality, interests, motivations and attitudes are very good at showing the 'red flags', who not to hire. They are not overly reliable in highlighting 'superstars'.

— Just because the person has been recommended or you know them socially is no substitute for understanding 'the real person'. Always check out the 'roots'.

— Using assessment is suitable for ALL job roles — it's a matter of choosing the appropriate tool for sa pecific job.

— Recruiting new staff is an expensive and time–consuming project. You can dramatically decrease these variables by using a pre–screening assessment right up front, thus not wasting time by interviewing numerous people who are not a good 'job fit'. We suggest CLUES.

— If 'selecting in' (i.e. you have cut your applicant pool to a final two or three), use a more in–depth system. We suggest ASSESS, Prevue or SalesMax.

— Improve your predictive validity by benchmarking, testing high performers and/or doing our Job Description survey (Prevue). This will ensure greater 'job fit'.

— Where applicable, do a Work Sample Test.

— Where there are big safety issues, a drug test may also be advisable, or the CLUES Attitude Test.

— Take a FREE test drive, contact us now.

—Also use profiling to understand existing employees' strengths and weaknesses. It cuts training costs considerably and makes training more efficient.

NO MORE SQUARE PEGS

7. INTERVIEWS

Step 5: Conducting the main interview

A study by the University of Toledo demonstrated that a group of interviewers had, for the most part, made up their mind within 15 seconds of meeting the candidate. That's as long as it takes for the parties to sit down!

Business leaders always promote the hiring and retaining of talent as the key to success. But most managers are less 'scientific' about hiring their 'greatest resource' than they are when buying a piece of office equipment. Too often they replace rigorous analysis and referencing with instant impressions, emotion and gut feel.

Every day I see managers basing the results of an interview on what the candidate looks like — Manners and Expressiveness, plus what they can do — Knowledge, Skills, Training, Experience, Education.

The job interview is the most popular assessment tool in the hiring process despite the fact that it is the most time consuming and therefore most expensive, plus the most unreliable predictor of job success and therefore the most dangerous.

Most hiring managers conduct unstructured interviews. These are basically a general 'get to know you' chit chat. This form of interview is highly unreliable and runs the risk of the interviewer asking questions that are not legally defensible because they are not aligned to the job. The unstructured interview also allows the candidate to answer questions with an opinion. Unstructured interviews are not consistent and are wide open to personal bias.

The unstructured interview ranks the lowest of any assessment measure in the selection process! Its validity is about .15 — that means about one in every six interviews will accurately identify a solid performer — very poor statistics.

Usually, short–listed applicants are invited to an interview. Some organisations use a telephone interview to check details in addition to the Application Form and CV as a screening tool. Doing so helps to reduce the shortlist. Its purpose, as discussed earlier, is to filter out those applicants who don't meet the minimum requirements for the job.

There are many types of interviews ranging from loosely structured one on one conversational interviews, to highly structured panel interviews. The purpose of an interview is to collect information that will show to what extent the applicant has the knowledge, skills, abilities, and personal attributes applicable to the role. Effective interviewing therefore depends on the type of questions that are asked and how they are interpreted and rated.

Do not use vague, unstructured questions such as:
- Tell me about yourself.
- How would your previous employer describe you?
- What are your career goals?
- What are your strengths and weaknesses?

These types of non–specific open–ended questions invite answers that are based on opinions. It is easy for the interviewee to give you an opinion about anything. What we are looking for is examples of past behaviour, as this will be a good indication of future behaviour.

A good employment interview is built around the 6 to 8 core performance factors (competencies) required for the position refer back to Chapter 4. Usually the development of one structured interview question and follow–up probe is sufficient for each performance factor. The structure of these questions can be behavioural, situational or knowledge based. Usually the knowledge–based questions are answered earlier in the hiring process via the contents of the application form and CV. These are then cross–checked in the telephone screen.

Types of interview questions

Behavioural questions: these will reveal how an applicant has responded and behaved in past situations. They always start with, 'tell me about a time . . .' or 'give me an example of what you did . . .' etc.

In a structured interview, applicants are asked to explain how they used the performance factors referred to above, in past jobs. For example, an essential performance factor for most positions is the ability to plan and organise. Examples of appropriate behavioural–based interview questions to assess this ability are:

❐ Describe to me how you organise your day to ensure you complete all your tasks? (Listen for a system). When does this system fail you and why?

❐ Tell me about a time when a colleague asked for help while you were in the middle of a very important task? What did you do?

❐ Think about a major project you completed recently. Can you please describe how you commenced and progressed this project in respect to ensuring all tasks were done on time and within budget?

Situational questions: these ask how applicants would respond to a specific situation. These questions usually start with 'what would you do...?' or 'how would you react to...?' etc.

If it is unlikely that the applicant has had past experience on a particular performance factor, then situational questions can be used. Examples of situation questions for the performance factor of Customer Service are:

❏ What would you do if a customer complained to you about the quality of service he received?

❏ Your manager has asked you to stay for the next shift as there is a large customer inflow, but you have a prior arrangement. What would your response be?

❏ A customer wants to purchase a product in stock, but desires a different colour. How would you respond?

Knowledge questions: these ask applicants about their understanding and knowledge on specific aspects of the job. These questions usually start with, 'do you know...?' or 'what experience do you have...?' etc.

Examples of knowledge questions:

❏ Can you use Microsoft Office applications?

❏ Do you know MYOB?

❏ How would you diagnose the timing on a 2006 Subaru?

Note: Most knowledge questions are irrelevant as this information is contained in the Application Form or CV. Check this first. Many managers waste valuable interview time asking questions that have already been answered in written form earlier.

It is also easy for a candidate to answer 'yes' to a knowledge question. It is good practice to validate this knowledge with a Work Sample or Skills Test. Reference and background checking will also highlight any knowledge gaps.

Unlawful questions

In terms of the Human Rights Act and the Employment Relations Act it is unlawful to discriminate, when employing staff, in terms of the applicant's:

Colour	Race
Gender	Ethnic or national origin
Age	Marital and family status
Disability	Religious or ethical belief
Political opinion	Employment status
Sexual orientation	Union involvement

Unlawful questions were addressed in more detail in Chapter 5 — Initial Screening.

Unless it is inherent in the position, don't ask it

There is a popular perception that it is illegal to ask *any* personal questions. This is not true.

The principle is that you cannot ask irrelevant questions and then discriminate against a person based on those irrelevant points.

Usually, but by no means always, personal questions are irrelevant. For instance, religion is irrelevant in performing most occupations, unless, for example, you are a priest (the law does not intend to force a congregation to appoint a person from another religion as their spiritual leader). In that case the need for a particular religious belief (and therefore discrimination against other religions) is based on the genuine occupational qualifications for the position. Other examples are age (certain jobs cannot be done by persons under a certain age, for example, bar work), or gender (for example, male actors for male parts in a play, women in sales positions for a lingerie shop).

The best advice is, if in doubt, leave it out!

Good Questions + Good Listening Skills = Successful Interviewing

---

Listening skills

The key to successful interviewing is having the right mix of questions and listening actively — talk 20% of the time, listen 80%. Active listening involves responding both verbally and non–verbally to the applicant, letting them know that you are giving them your full attention.

Hiring managers tend to spend too much time selling the virtues of the company, the job and its promotional opportunities and not enough time evaluating the candidate's ability to deliver on the performance factors required for the job. As an interviewer, your job is to extract as much information in the allotted time frame to make a sound hiring (or not to hire) decision.

You can only achieve this by actively listening!

Active listening involves:

❏ Paraphrasing to state in your own words what you think the person has said.

❏ Asking probing questions to indicate interest and clarify understanding.

❏ Using appropriate non–verbal communication like making

eye contact, nodding your head and showing interest.

When communicating we depend heavily on non–verbal communication, in fact:

> **Body language = 55% of communication**
> **Speech tone = 38% of communication**
> **Words = 7% of communication**

Preparing for an interview

Employment interviews can be intimidating for both parties. It is imperative that you are well prepared prior to the interview meeting.

As a busy manager it's easy to lose track of time, suddenly realising you have an interview meeting in 10 minutes. Under–prepared managers will wing it or, worse still, live under the illusion that no prepared questions are necessary as they are very good at 'reading' people through a simple social chit chat.

Being prepared means understanding the six to eight core performance factors (competencies) required for the job and linking a behavioural interview question to each one.

Make sure you also re–read the employee profile and extrapolate one or two question (given in the profile) to help you validate any strengths or weaknesses in the assessment.

Another advantage of preparation is the image created with the candidate. It positions you and your company in a professional light.

Getting started

Greet the candidate by name and shake hands. Introduce yourself and give your title. Although they may not show it the candidate will be nervous, so break the ice by engaging in some small talk to relax the person (and yourself). To make a quality hiring decision you want to extract as much information during the interview as time permits.

Nervous people do not provide quality information.

During the interview it is important for one interviewer to be assigned to take notes. This can be off–putting to the interviewee who may feel they have answered a question in the negative if they see an interviewer immediately putting pen to paper.

For this reason it is best practice to inform the candidate that you will be taking notes during the interview as a matter of record.

Finally, advise the candidate that following your questions they will have the opportunity to interview you — to ask any questions relating to the job and your organisation.

Controlling the interview

If you are getting the information you want and all is progressing well, then controlling techniques aren't necessary.

However if the candidate is avoiding your questions, trying to take control from you or giving opinions, then some techniques to prevent wasting time are useful.

These techniques include:

❐ Asking close–ended questions.

❐ Referring to the time you have allowed for the interview.

❐ Politely interrupting the applicant and asking a job–related question.

Closing the interview

Before closing the interview, give the applicant an opportunity to ask any questions they may have regarding the position or the company.

Once these have been answered, close the interview by:

❑ Reviewing the key responsibilities of the position.

❑ Addressing salary, hours of work, benefits, holidays etc. Note, this should have been done at the Application/telephone interview stage as some of these points are strong knock outs and it's a great waste of management time to get to this final step only to have the candidate say 'no' because she did know she had to work weekends.

❑ Reviewing the next steps in the selection process — be precise here. 'We will be contacting you next Wednesday morning to inform you if we wish to move you forward in the process, or to advise you that you have been unsuccessful.'

❑ Some organisations then give the candidate a worksite tour. This has its advantages and disadvantages. On the downside it is a waste of time if you have several interviews and perhaps the next interviewed person will be a better prospect than the previous.

It may also give the candidate an unrealistic perception that the job is probably theirs.

The advantage is that it gives the candidate a realistic preview of the work environment with the added benefit of 'selling' the candidate on the job

❑ Walk the person out.

Even if during the interview you assess that the applicant does not have the required skill set it is important that you continue with the interview, to ensure that all applicants are treated consistently.

NO MORE SQUARE PEGS

8. EVALUATING INTERVIEWS

Step 5: Evaluating interview answers

A good response to a behavioural question follows the SOAR principle.

The applicant outlines:

☐ The **S**ituation which he or she was in.

☐ The **O**bjectives to be achieved.

☐ The **A**ctions taken.

☐ The **R**esults obtained.

To ensure that all applicants' responses are evaluated against the same benchmark it is valuable to develop Behavioural Rating Guides for assessing responses to questions.

These rating guides also enable you to assess the response, making it easier to compare applicants.

Unacceptable	Acceptable	Superior
1 2	**3**	**4 5**
Does not listen to others. Is overly dependent on others. Is critical of others.	Listens to others. Is prepared to help others when asked.	Communicates in an open manner. Offers help and support. Is positive towards others.

Always have the interview team score the candidate immediately after the interview has concluded — do this without fail. A rating guide that includes specific behaviours will minimise bias. Interviewers often fall prey to the following biases:

❒ Central tendency bias — giving a middle rating to all performance factors — giving the benefit of the doubt, or having a 'bob each way'.

❒ Leniency/strictness bias — consistently giving either only high or only low ratings. This is usually influenced by the interviewer's personality characteristics. For example, highly aggressive and assertive managers are more critical and rate harder as opposed to, say, managers that are more diplomatic and cooperative, who may be more lenient.

❒ Halo–effect bias — this is the most common interview bias —letting one factor (e.g. hobbies, sports, acquaintances) influence everything else. The halo effect overlaps with first impression. Imagine the manager is a keen yachtie and the candidate an ex–America's Cup sailor. We like people who are like ourselves and likability is a big persuader. This is linked to the similarity bias. This is the key reason why interviews should be structured and conducted by more than one person. This lessens the chance of allowing personal factors to influence the interview outcome.

❒ Contrast effect — assessing applicant in relation to the applicants previously interviewed. A common but flawed practice is to set a day or half–day aside and attack the interview process in one hit. This format puts the manager in danger of positioning the first interviewee as the benchmark that subsequent interviewees are measured against. To eliminate this bias, space your interviews, say one a day, or one in the early morning and the second late in the day. If you have followed my previous steps and screened out efficiently, you probably only have two to four people to interview. You need to concentrate on evaluating, 'does this person have the required SKAMPE for the role?' Not, 'how does she compare to that last candidate?'

❏ First impression, making a decision in the first few minutes of the interview — it's human nature. We are innately wired to judge people as soon as we meet them. In psychology we call this the Fight or Flight Syndrome. Based on animal behaviour, we are wired to instantly assess — do we stay and be prepared to fight, or do we remove ourselves from the situation?

This instant judgement is usually based on appearance and mannerisms. After all, in the first few minutes of meeting someone, these two characteristics are all we have on which to base our judgement.

Making decisions about future job performance based on appearance and manners is very dangerous. Just because a person looks good and is polite doesn't mean they can do the job well.

❏ Biases and stereotypes — This is linked to first impressions. Allowing personal biases to influence ratings of applicants is common amongst interviewers. This is usually based on the interviewer's personal values. For example, a dislike of tattoos, earrings on men, shaved heads, short–sleeved shirts etc. often leads the interviewer to form judgements (positive or negative) based on appearance and not on what the candidate can do.

❏ Overly sensitive to negative information. Many interviewers look for reasons to reject rather than a reason to hire. Again this can be linked to personal biases and values. Likewise, interviewers can be overly sensitive to one positive piece of information, or to appearance, which are often linked to first impression.

Effective interview checklist

❐ Ensure you are not interrupted for the duration of the interview. Take the phone off the hook, put a 'do not disturb' sign on the door.

❐ Open the interview in a warm and friendly manner. Engage in some light social banter. Develop rapport with the applicant, putting them at ease by allowing for a few minutes of small talk.

❐ Now set up the ground rules. 'I will ask some questions. What I require are some concrete examples of what you did, not opinions. We will also be taking some notes; this does not signal incorrect or poor answers. And finally, after our questions we will give you the opportunity to question us'.

❐ Listen actively and openly to the applicant's responses. Use the 80/20 rule — let the applicant do 80% of the talking and you do 20%.

❐ Don't finish the applicant's answers. Use probing questions to extract more information.

❐ Focus on what the applicant says; not on their appearance (unless of course appearance is a performance factor — sales assistant in a beauty parlour!).

❐ Stay focused, demonstrate you're listening, and be attentive. Use body language to indicate engagement — nodding your head, eye contact etc.

❐ View the applicant's responses neutrally and not emotionally (this may be difficult, but simply being aware of your own reactions is a great help).

❐ Take notes. Don't ask questions that are not legally defensible, e.g. questions related to gender, religion, race, culture, marital status, age, disability, organisational affiliations, or arrests.

Double checking

Since CVs and interviews can be manipulated to create a particular impression it is useful to once again review the insights gathered from the job–fit assessment and work samples. These assessments and work samples should not replace interviews, but rather supplement them.

A great deal of research and scientific evidence demonstrates interview reliability and validity can be increased by concentrating on these six key areas:

❒ Train interviewers.

❒ Ask the same behavioural questions (based on the job competencies) to all candidates.

❒ Do job analyses before you begin the hiring process.

❒ Gather salient prior information.

❒ Make sure you rate each area of the selection process — particularly the interview — and make your ratings descriptive — i.e. exceeds, meets, does not meet etc. (job requirements).

❒ Always use two or more interviewers.

Step Five Reminders . . .

— Be prepared. Always go into an interview with a printed list of questions based on the job's performance factors.

— Develop a set of two questions for each performance factor. Usually one question from each factor is sufficient.

— Ensure all questions are lawful.

— Always use a structured interview based on behavioural or situational questions. Remember, past behaviour reflects future behaviour.

— Every candidate must be asked the same questions.

— Remember, you are looking for concrete examples of past performance, not opinions.

— Have one person take notes.

— Immediately after the interview, have the team 'score' the candidate's performance against the performance factors — use a tracking sheet.

— Always have two or more people conduct the interview.

— Let the candidate speak 80% of the time, you 20% — Listen, listen, listen.

— Control the interview. Don't let candidates wander off the subject or give opinions.

— At the end of your interview, allow candidates to ask you questions.

On conclusion, tell the candidate what will happen next and be specific.

9. REFERENCE CHECKING

Step 6: Reference and background checking

Since employment is a long–term commitment it pays to remember that often, when you act in haste, you save enough time to repent at leisure. Make sure that you do a reference check on an applicant before offering them a position. It is often advisable to do this before the main interview. You may quickly discover some negatives that will 'knock out' the candidate before you waste valuable management time on an expensive and often invalid interview.

The purpose of a reference check is to validate the information that you have gathered on the applicant during the selection process. As this is sometimes a time–consuming process many employers take a shortcut by failing to do a reference check. This can be a fatal and costly decision.

Some employers are loath to give information about past employees. There are several strategies to help extract valid information.

Structuring the reference checks will increase the accuracy of your information:

❏ Confirm the information provided by the applicant, such as employment dates.

❏ Get the referees' views of the applicant in terms of the

essential performance factors (e.g. sales ability, attention to detail etc.) Ask them to rate the applicant on a scale from excellent to good, fair, and poor.

Other questions you could consider are:

❏ How did this person perform relative to other people in this position?

❏ Would you re–employ them if you had an opening?

❏ Why did they leave your company?

❏ The applicant is applying for XYZ position; in your opinion is he/she qualified and able to do the job?

❏ What was their attendance like?

❏ Did they respect company property?

❏ Any other comments that would help us in our assessment of this person?

Fake references

We all know that job candidates embellish, enhance, exaggerate — call it what you will — to make their CV and themselves more appealing to hiring managers. There has been a great deal of research into the extent of lying in CVs. Figures run between 53% and 68% with college graduates being the worst at 70%. Many of these 'little white lies' are not caught by managers, and providing the employee wasn't a complete disaster on the job, nobody is ever the wiser.

But in these tougher times competition in the job market has driven many candidates to desperate measures. Little white lies have now turned into works of total fiction. Enter CareerExcuse. com. Here is an outfit that will create a complete work history for a job candidate. From their side, they create a 'real' company with address, website and free phone number, and 'real' managers and referees. So when a prospective employer calls to verify work history and performance everything the applicant told you checks out and the feedback is glowing! Blown away? It seems unbelievable, but it is true. Try it yourself.

As managers, our saving grace is that not all candidates are going to go to these extremes — the low fee may scare the jobless off. However, for those with small budgets and no scruples there is another service — FakeResumes.com. This is more of a 'tips' site to give candidates techniques on how to get around employment gaps, lack of experience etc. They claim to reveal 'the main reason good liars get job offers and honest people don't!'

Over the last 10 years of helping managers set up structured hiring systems, I've seen it all. I am afraid I have become rather cynical of what I read in CVs and hear from reference sources given by candidates. As New Zealanders we are a nation of very trusting people. This is part of our charm and why tourists love this country. But when it comes to hiring, this wonderful trait ends up biting us on the rear end.

When it comes to reference–checking candidates, busy managers tend to 'satisfice.' They look for the first sufficiently satisfactory reference as a 'go' signal. If the CV reads well, the given references sound great and the person 'fronts up' well, they must be able to do the job. Wrong! Remember, the candidate you see at interview is the best you will ever see them — you're the audience and they are the actors on the stage.

There is only one way to beat these impostors — due diligence before you start your reference. When it comes to hiring, most managers are not diligent which can be much to their detriment later on.

Here are some simple examples of how you can verify applicant work history prior to referencing:

1 Does the company exist? Do a Google search, check sites like LinkedIn, and also Chamber of Commerce membership etc.

2 Cross reference the telephone number given against previous employers. If there is a mobile number call it and request a landline number to call back. There's a great scam where the telephone number given is that of a mate.

3 Search for the candidate in LinkedIn and on other sites. This can give valuable information on work history and associates you can use to cross reference what you see in the CV.

4 Use pre–employment screening tests. Besides 'job fit' based on personality, mental ability and attitude, these also have a faking scale that highlights candidates trying to 'paint' themselves up to be better than they really are. Whilst this may not be a 'knock out' in itself, one would have to ask that if they 'fake' during a psychometric profile, wouldn't they also do this in their CV and interview? To use the baseball analogy, one strike–out is benefit of the doubt — three is definitely out.

5 Be fair. Former employers and co–workers can make mistakes. Sometimes companies may have gone out of business. Many times there are individual conflicts that override a positive recommendation based on work ability. Revisit the candidate and give them an opportunity to explain.

6 Use common sense. If it walks like a duck and quacks like a duck it's likely it is a duck!

Put on your 'cynical' hat — don't leap to conclusions. Take your time to complete due diligence. Check and then re–check because what you see and hear is not necessarily all factual and therefore what you end up paying for.

In view of the Privacy Act, always obtain the applicant's consent before approaching referees or other sources. I like to try and make this as broad as possible — 'Can I contact any supervisors/managers in you past positions to ask about your work ethic?'

Reference Checking Form

Introduce yourself, and explain reasons for the call — '(Name) has applied for the position of (give details of job and your company). They have suggested you as a referee to their application. Do you have about 15 minutes to talk now, or shoud I call back when it's more convenient?'

Candidate and referee details

Date of reference check	
Candidate	
Referee	
Company	*Tel:*
Relationship to applicant	
Dates of employment	*Start:* *End:*
Type of employment	*Permanent:* *Contract:*
Candidate's role when employed by referee's company	

Above and overleaf: A sample of a reference checking form that can be adapted for your own needs

Performance factors

'Please describe the applicant's performance with regards to the following categories:' Rate the applicant based on the referee's answers.

1. *List your top–ranked performance factor (see page 74) here:*

Unsatisfactory	Below average	Average	Above average	Outstanding

2. *List your second–ranked performance factor here:*

Unsatisfactory	Below average	Average	Above average	Outstanding

3. *List your third–ranked performance factor here:*

Unsatisfactory	Below average	Average	Above average	Outstanding

4. *List your fourth–ranked performance factor here:*

Unsatisfactory	Below average	Average	Above average	Outstanding

5. *List fifth top–ranked performance factor here:*

Unsatisfactory	Below average	Average	Above average	Outstanding

Applicant descriptions

Were there any problems with health or absenteeism?

Did they have consideration for company property?

Why did the applicant leave your company?

Would you re–employ him/her? If no, why not?

What were the applicant's strengths?

Are there any areas that you felt he/she might need training for?

The candidate is being considered for a (position) role. In your opinion is he/she qualified to do the job?

Overall performance

How well were you satisfied with the applicant's efforts and achievements?

Unsatisfactory	Below average	Average	Above average	Outstanding

Is there any other information a prospective employer should know about the applicant?

Background checks

In certain positions, for example where large amounts of money are handled, it is also necessary to do other relevant checks, such as credit checks, convictions etc. The Department of Courts can be contacted for information on previous criminal convictions.

There are also specific organisations that will conduct these background checks at a very reasonable fee, e.g. debt collection companies, private investigators, security companies or organisations that specialise in employment screening. We recommend Personal Verification Ltd.

A final thought on references

If a referee provides information on an applicant on a confidential basis, a request for access to information by the applicant at a later date may be refused in terms of the Privacy Act on the basis that it is evaluative material.

REFERENCE CHECKING

Employees will rarely supply a referee that will give a bad reference. Always seek alternatives. Ask, 'I note you have the sales manager down as a referee. Would the accountant know your work? Can we talk to him/her?'

Step Six Reminders ...

— Always do a reference checks. Ensure these are from individuals that have previously managed the candidate, NOT family and friends.

— Cross validate the contents of the Application Form, the candidate's knowledge, skill and experience and any weaknesses highlighted in the employee profile with referees.

— Ask the candidate's permission to use any reference points that are not on the CV.

— Usually, reference contacts on a CV are not reliable. Would you put a referee on your CV who will give you a bum wrap?

— Use referencing to validate what you have seen in the employment test.

— Depending on job role, consider doing a background check using a suitable specialised agency. This helps identify criminal activity, credit problems, bogus qualifications etc.

NO MORE SQUARE PEGS

10. CHOOSING THE BEST PERSON

Step 7: How to pick the best applicant

Once you have gone through all the stages of the selection process, systematically filtering the applicants in terms of the essential and desirable performance factors, a final selection decision can be made.

Hopefully one or two applicants have come through the process head and shoulders above the others.

In this situation the hard decision will be to decide which of the applicants best match the essential and desirable performance factors and what other bonus performance factors each applicant has.

Remember that you do not have to make an appointment. If your assessment is that none of the applicants meets the essential and desirable performance factors, then it would be best to start your search again.

Do not get caught in the trap of 'hiring the best of a bad bunch'!

Also, if circumstances change during the selection process and you have not made an offer, you can terminate the process.

Simply let the applicants know that due to unforeseen circumstances the position has fallen away.

Rejecting applicants

In the hurdle approach to selection, applicants are systematically 'knocked out' at each stage. Those applicants that have not made it through to the next stage should be sent a letter informing them that they have not been successful. This process is very important — remember that every person that you reject may be a potential customer.

The way in which the rejection process is handled directly affects the image of your company. The rejection letter should be brief and to the point. You are not required to explain why you did not appoint. Getting sucked into this conversation can cause problems and in some cases a personal grievance claim!

Offering the position

Once a decision has been made to hire an applicant it is important to clarify the terms and conditions that you will offer the person. Be sure that you do want to offer the person the position before contacting them, as a verbal offer of employment can be enforced.

So either put the offer in writing or present the offer in terms of an offer for discussion. The applicant may wish to seek independent advice about the agreement and its terms.

The contract and any bargaining around the offer has to take into account the Employment Relations Act of 2000 and any collective employment agreement that is in place in your workplace.

Ensure that the contract is signed before the person starts work.

Storing the selection information

Information gathered during the selection process should

not be kept after that process has concluded. If it is to be used for another purpose, the person concerned has to agree beforehand.

Avoid costly mistakes

Selecting the right staff is fundamental to the success of your company. Mistakes are extremely costly. So remember:

❒ The nature of the future relationship between the employer and employee will depend on the extent to which both parties have acted in good faith and have been open and honest in their interactions.

❒ The privacy and confidentiality of the applicant has to be maintained throughout the process.

❒ The selection techniques and tools used must be accurate, fair, legally defensible and cost effective.

Some concluding thoughts

❒ You will not get 'readable' results from any part of the selection process from anxious and nervous candidates. Always try to establish a relaxing rapport. Address this issue up front.

❒ Always have one person take notes during the interview.

❒ Control the interview. Avoid small talk and caution the candidate that you want real life examples to your interview questions, not opinions.

❒ During the interview ask one question at a time, repeating it if necessary. Follow up with a probing question.

❒ During the interview, Listen, Listen, Listen.

❒ Observe body actions. This will tell you if the candidate is nervous. If so, stop the interview and address this issue — settle the candidate down and recommence interview.

❒ At the end of the interview, allow the candidate to question you about your company and the position.

❐ Don't oversell the position. Most employees who leave within three to six months do so because they thought the job was going to be different.

❐ Selection is a two–way process. Remember, whilst we want to hire tough and manage easy, employees in today's market do have choices.

❐ Always communicate the next step in the process and stick to that. Be wary of candidates who try to 'hold a gun to your head' — 'I need a decision now as I have two other jobs on hold.'

Step Seven Reminders . . .

— Don't select the best from a bad bunch. Be prepared to start again.

— Advise all unsuccessful candidates immediately.

— Ensure your employment agreement and/or contracts are signed off before the person starts work.

— Instigate an induction programme.

— Start an employee appraisal programme from day one.

Checklist for using select–in approach

Step 1: Analyse the job

☐ Review present
position description
☐ Observe position
☐ Interview person
presently in position
☐ Write position
description
☐ Identify key
performance factors

Person responsible ✓

Step 2: Recruit applicants

☐ Decide whether to
recruit yourself or use
an agency. If doing the
recruiting yourself . . .
☐ Write an
advertisement
☐ Decide where to
advertise
☐ Appoint an administrator
to process applicants

Person responsible ✓

Step 3: Initial screening

☐ Review CVs
☐ Conduct telephone
interviews, if applicable
☐ Send rejection letters

Person responsible ✓

Step 4: Employee Testing

❒ Choose appropriate employment tests
❒ Prepare applicant for testing (lower anxiety by explaining process)
❒ If testing on site, arrange a quiet test space
❒ Conduct all tests in a standardised manner
❒ Send rejection letters

Person responsible ✓

Work sample (optional)

❒ Ask the applicant to complete a work sample, e.g. presentation
❒ Send rejection letters

Drug testing (optional, depending on role)

Step 5: Interviewing

❒ Arrange interview venue and times, allowing at least one hour per interview. Be prepared to schedule some interviews outside of work hours
❒ Choose appropriate interviewers (at least two)
❒ Contact applicants to arrange date, time and venue for interview

Person responsible ✓

SUMMARY CHECKLIST

☐ Review the position
description and develop
appropriate interview
questions (the same for
all applicants)
☐ Ensure all interviewers
have reviewed the
applicant's application
form and CV and
are familiar with the
performance factors and
interview questions
☐ Decide on the seating
arrangements
☐ Assign someone to
open the interview
☐ Assign interview
questions to specific
interviewers
☐ Assign someone to
take notes throughout
the interview
☐ Assign someone to
close the interview
☐ Ensure you have all
the relevant details
pertaining to the position
on hand (e.g. salary
range, leave, hours,
benefits, overtime)
☐ Send rejection letters

Step 6: Reference/
background check
☐ Conduct reference and
background checks
☐ Send rejection letters

Person responsible   ✓

Step 7: Make an offer

☐ Make an offer of employment to applicants who have successfully met all the performance factors (established in Step 1)
☐ Ensure employment contract is signed
☐ Conduct induction training
☐ Begin a performance management process

Person responsible   ✓

'Enjoy the satisfaction of knowing you have made a good decision, immediately and into the future, as the selected candidate's performance and work record proves you right.'

DEFINITIONS

Some terms used in this book may not be familiar to you. Here are some brief definitions.

Abilities: These are the foundation for learning skills. They measure the potential of an individual to perform a particular job based on mental ability (how quick do they 'get it'?) and physical skills (can they lift 20kgs on a regular basis?). Throughout this book I am more inclined to use the terminology 'mental ability'.

Attitude: (or Counter Productive Behaviours): Closely aligned to Values — Values drive attitudes that are reflected in behaviour. Attitudes are also aligned to an individual's integrity. Attitudes are measured in areas like honesty, workplace aggression, attitudes to drugs and alcohol, sexual harassment, computer abuse, punctuality etc.

Attributes: Usually used to describe the broad characteristics of a person in relationship to that individual's personality — their innate characteristics and/or traits.

Behavioural–based Interview: Interviews (questions) in which applicants describe how they would perform in certain situations — based on the theory that past behaviour suggests future behaviour.

Cognitive Tests: Aligned to ability tests used to measure different aspects of intelligence, such as inductive and the duct of reasoning, Emery and mathematical reasoning.

Competencies: A competency is a set of knowledge, skills, experience, attributes and abilities that the incumbent needs to bring to a position in order to perform its tasks and functions with competence (Woodruffe, 1992).

Correlation: Measure of the extent to which two variables are related — remember the relationship is not necessarily one of cause and effect.

Experience: A person's work history and qualifications — how much experience have they gained in relationship to the skills required for this role?

Halo effect: When raters or managers base performance as being good or bad solely on the basis of one specific factor

Job analysis: A procedure for identifying the duties or behaviours that define a job.

Job description: Information about all aspects of the job.

Job fit: Every person has a right to work and every job requires the right person. Hiring new staff is about ensuring the hired person is the right 'fit' for the specific role they are applying for. This is to the benefit of both parties.

Knowledge: What the person needs to know and understand to effectively perform the required work, e.g. university knowledge of financial theory. Measure knowledge through the CV, verify it through reference and background checks.

Mental abilities: Often referred to as Mental Ability: how capable the person is of understanding and learning new tasks, and of drawing conclusions and formulating strategies, e.g. above–average numerical ability as measured by numerical abilities tests. This is akin to intelligence.

DEFINITIONS

Multi–rated interview: A structured interview conducted by two or more persons with the answer of each question being scored by the interviewer.

Personality attributes: Defined as a dynamic and organized set of characteristics possessed by a person that uniquely influences his or her thinking/feelings, motivations, and behaviors in various situations. They are a set of personal characteristics that reflect how a person typically deals with his or her world. These areas are measured through personality profiling.

Reliability (of test results): Refers to consistency — if we were to measure a candidate today and then in six months time we would expect the scores to be similar. If not the test is not reliable and therefore is not valid.

Skill: What the person must be able to do and demonstrate to effectively perform the required work. Skill reflects a level of proficiency (usually aligned to experience) in applying knowledge (e.g. proficiency at completing numerical problems). Skills can be technical (e.g. welding), or non–technical (e.g. negotiating skills).

Structured interview: A procedure in which all applicants are asked the same questions.

Validity (test): The correspondence between a measurement gained through an employment test and the actual attribute and/or ability to test is measuring.

Work–sample testing: A method to assess applicants knowledge, skill and experience for a particular job task by getting applicant to perform that task.

Bibliography & references

Cook, M. (1998), *Personnel Selection*. Chichester. Wiley.

Greenberg, H & Greenberg, J. (1985), Job Matching For Better Sales Performance. *Harvard Business Review*, Vol.58, No. 5.

Landy, F.J. (1980), Stamp collecting vs science. *American Psychologist*, November, 1183 — 92.

Mount, M K & Barrick, M R (1995), The Big Five personality dimensions: implications for research and practice in human resources management. *Research in Personnel and Human Resources Management,* 13, 153200.

Smith, M. & Smith, P. (2005), *Testing People at Work*. Oxford. Blackwell.

Acknowledgements

Most of us can remember our favourite schoolteacher. When we reflect, the reason was because we actually enjoyed learning what they taught us — they were genuinely good teachers. In 1995 I went 'back to school' full-time and one of my lecturers was Dr Hillary Bennett. She was not only my favourite teacher, but in 2000 became my business partner when we launched AssessSystems.

This book is based a compilation of the many articles Hillary and I wrote on the hiring process, so I'd like to thank her for teaching me so well and, in an indirect way, contributing to this subject matter.

Also, thanks to Peter Jessup whose journalistic skills whipped my completed prose into shape, Geoff Moore who gave me plenty of spelling lessons and my publisher, Josh Easby, who not only guided this whole project, but also designed and formatted this book — a man of many talents. Thanks, Josh!